Reel Life Behind the Screen

Reel Life Behind the Screen

A Cinema Manager Remembers

A memoir by
Nick Scudamore

Matador
Unit E2 Airfield Business Park,
Harrison Road, Market Harborough,
Leicestershire. LE16 7UL
Tel: 0116 2792299
Email: books@troubador.co.uk
Web: www.troubador.co.uk/matador
Twitter: @matadorbooks

Original design by Inajara Schuaber Gomes

ISBN 978 1 80313 332 4

British Library Cataloguing in Publication Data.
A catalogue record for this book is available from the British Library.

Printed and bound by CPI Group (UK) Ltd, Croydon, CR0 4YY
Typeset in 11pt Minion Pro by Troubador Publishing Ltd, Leicester, UK

Matador is an imprint of Troubador Publishing Ltd

To Pauline F and Susan K

whose sustained encouragement then and now remains,
as ever, essential. N.

The information on the history of individual cinemas has been sourced from:

Kensington and Chelsea Local Studies and Archives, www.rbkc.gov.uk/libraries
Islington Local History Centre, www.islington.gov.uk/heritage
Camden Local Studies and Archives, www.camden.gov.uk/libraries
The Cinema Theatre Association, cinema-theatre.org.uk
Cinema Treasures, cinematreasures.org
Historic England Archive, www.ukcinemas.org.uk
Wikipedia

Thanks to all donors and contributors to these.

A CAVEAT

The text that follows makes no claim to be history, nor does it pretend to be fiction. It is simply a memoir, based on the imperfect records of memory alone. Some names have been changed as a courtesy and some details compressed for fluency of narrative. But always the intention has been to write down what I remember of what I felt at the time.

Contents

Scudamore Bookshop, Earl's Court 1970

James Scudamore started *Scudamore Books Ltd* in about 1957. It closed in 1979.

Pastel by John Foley (1917–2011).

The artist was a distinguished neurologist and friend of the Scudamore family.

Private Collection

Earl's Court, Summer 1978

For a long time, I used to go to bed late. Coming home from the cinema in the evening I would always write my diary card. For years I used to keep an alphabetical card index of every film I saw. Some nights I would write up as many as three cards, 4x6", both sides, in brown ink.

Have you ever considered what happens when you go to a cinema to see the latest release? You pay your money, you sit, you watch, you leave. Yet the process to achieve this effect has changed so much in the last forty years or so that it would be in many ways almost unrecognisable to a customer from 1979. For example, most cinemas don't have need of a projectionist with traditional skills anymore. The film is supplied on what is effectively a very large data-stick, with the film and adverts downloaded onto it, which is attached to the projector and an operator presses 'play'. This is seen as much cheaper and more efficient for both the distributor (the company that supplies the film to the cinema) and the cinema owners. The old, perforated film strip hasn't disappeared entirely, but since the end of 2015 this hundred-year-old-technology of celluloid-on-a-reel has become an extreme rarity in most of the developed world.

The whole commercial model for cinema-going has now changed beyond recognition. Hollywood ceased expecting to make the bulk of its earning from cinema exhibition as early as the mid-nineties. By then television, VHS tape, both in rental and sell-through publishing, along with cable TV, airline rentals, and foreign release sales accumulatively earned far more of the total take on any given new release title for the studios. Since then, we've added the far higher quality of DVD and Blu-Ray disc publishing, and in the last eight years or so online streaming of new feature films directly into our homes, our computers, our phones.

So traditional cinema-going, as a regular habit, belongs nowadays mainly to only two classes of people. The first are the well-to-do middle-class metropolitans who have discovered that their local small art cinema, in the unlikely event that it has survived at all, has now had an extensive make-over of both content and facilities. There is more comfortable seating, along with far more expensive but much more upscale drinks and snacks often brought direct to your seat. The specialist film-programming is nowadays often buttressed by an irregular programme of Q+A sessions with directors or writers – if ever such delicate creatures can be persuaded to attend an opening weekend. There are now also commonly high-priced special digitally streamed screenings of opera and theatre presentations on specific dates. It's a redesign of the cinema hall product for a much more specific market. Whether the Covid-19 pandemic will mark the death knell of the local cinema hall we shall all discover soon enough.

The other main group that still actually visit cinema halls is a hold-over from the old mass-market days: males from 14 to 25 years who, then as now, like to take dates to the pictures, so stories that involve plenty of explosions and screaming will draw them into the hall still. If these noisy titles can be designed to be tolerable to parents or younger teens in addition, then the chances of a Harry Potter / Jason Bourne type hit are much increased.

By contrast, the DVD purchase market for the youngest children has been the mainstay of that end of film business for several decades. Disney were the first to benefit from this, realising, as they did after some significant initial resistance but long before their rivals, that their cartoon and animal story feature films had a built in afterlife for every succeeding generation of children. Their cartoon versions of *Pinocchio* or *Cinderella* routinely appeared on specially selected cinema screens about every seven years. When it came to VHS, and then DVD, publication was the natural extension of this policy. Disney have long been sure to preserve their camera negatives in very good order so as to be able to strike new prints and to regularly re-release all their most popular titles in whatever new format is developed, as well as marketing a whole catalogue of new ancillary films and computer games for all their new titles. Naturally Disney has expanded into the streaming pay-per-view market with vigour and increasing success.

In 2022 there are still clear sub-sets within the surviving mass-market: chick-flicks and horror films being two of the most obvious examples. Again, the real profit anticipated here is repeat business at the first-run cinema which stokes the climate of desire, so that enthusiasts for a specific film will later purchase the subsequent DVD with additional commentary tracks. TV dramas have an equivalent afterlife also. After premiere cable transmission there are follow repeats, with a digital 'box set' to follow. Physical box sets of DVD discs currently still exist in 2022 but they are no longer a default option for a studio or rights holder. In sum, the traditional cinema hall has been slipping further and further from the centre of mass culture in all the decades since the late 1940s. And with the Covid-19 pandemic having mandated the temporary closing of the old halls for the best part of seventeen months the process of social habit away from a physical location for enjoying films has become greatly accelerated. Further, it's astounding to think that in 1979 neither the internet or mobile phones existed, at least not in the sense of being ubiquitous and essential to the ordering of daily life, as now. So, I intend to record in these pages just a little of what working in those nearly vanished cinemas was like, half a lifetime ago.

Like so many of the formative events of my life, becoming a cinema manager was an accident. Or at least an accident waiting to happen. I always loved a trip to the cinema. When I was a child TV had significant disadvantages: it was small and tinny, the pictures were in black and white, and my parents disapproved of it. But my father liked to take me to the pictures as a weekly outing. The picture there was huge and often in colour, the narrative almost always clear and compelling. I had been a sickly child since birth, having always what my grandmother referred to as 'a chest'. I was then, and remain today, a chronic sufferer from COPD (chronic obstructive pulmonary disease) always in need of much treatment. Perhaps back then my kindly father thought the cinema would be a useful diversion. A trip to the pictures was indeed often a useful palliative to the daily routines of physiotherapy and drugs.

In 1978 I had been out of graduate school a year or so. I was working at my father's antiquarian bookshop that was at the southern end of the Earl's Court Road in London, close to the Brompton Cemetery and along from the Earl's Court Arena. I had dreams of being a film editor at a film production house. I had no contacts, no clear idea how to go about the meetings that would lead to this profession, and not much concept of what a film editor actually did. I bought a copy of *Spotlight* – the actor's trade gazette – and looked up all the film companies on Wardour Street and then sent each one the same CV and covering letter. It's tempting to exaggerate, but I do believe I sent out over one hundred and fifty letters. Remember this was all well before the internet so such scatter-shot random activity was the conventional procedure. I got fewer than a dozen replies of any kind and only a single interview, and that one lasted about four minutes.

Dad had retired from his antiquarian bookshop some years before, compelled by declining health. My mother had taught herself the second-hand book trade as far as she was able and had run the shop, with a succession of lady friends helping her, for the best part of a decade. I had worked there already, during summer vacations from university. It wasn't heavy work, and within a certain frame of reference, actually quite stimulating. But then the lease on the shop came up for review and the new rent proposed by the landlords amounted to a five-fold increase. This immediately made running the shop utterly uneconomic. Mum had run it on the thinnest of shoestrings always, and if it never made much profit then at least the losses had always been manageably modest. Mum had always hoped that Dad's health would improve and that he would be able to take up the reins again. It had been a labour both of love and of hope for her. However, the days of the shop were now numbered, and I would have to look for some other way to earn pocket money while I found a profession.

New Manager for the Paris Pullman

foods, and letting the cinema out for big occasions, for which he can book special films, provide microphone and (minute) stage facilities, and a choice of I6 or 35ml. projection.

Contemporary Cinemas have plans to build a five storey building with two cinemas and twelve flats on the the sites of the Pullman and the house behind it, but they don't intend to do it in the immediate future. Meanwhile they're giving Kevin a free hand. When the new place is opened they'll follow the same policies as at present, using the second screen as a greater opportunity for experiment.

And what about Kevin's favourite films? 'The old ones,' he says, 'Hitchcock and Bogart.'

Nick Scudamore (left), RESPONSE film buff and assistant manager of the Paris Pullman hands over the Pullman's key to the new manager, Kevin Hibbitt.

Nick's off to Oxford where Contemporary Cinemas (who own the Pullman) have two cinemas for him to pour his skills into.

Kevin, aged 23, trained with EMI and ran Studios I,2 and 3 in Winchester for a year. He sees his first job as getting larger audiences for the main features.

After its most succesful year ever in I976 attendances have decreased, and he feels new life can be injected by the attitude of his staff. The last film, 'The Lacemaker' was certainly the best feature for many months. The new one is American: 'Stepford Wives', based on a book written by the same person as wrote 'Rosemary's Baby'.

Late night audiences have been solidly improving under Nick's guidance, and will now be taken over by Milena Rysova who was assistant manager in the days of big Jeff Curtis. 'I would like to see people write in and leave notes as to what they want on at their cinema' says Kevin.

Other intentions include the kiosk going over to all health

From *Response*, a community newsletter set up by Neil Bartlett.

Photograph of Nick Scudamore and Kevin Hibbitt outside the Paris Pullman, Chelsea 1979

By kind permission of Response Community Trust
www.responseprojects.org.uk

The *Response* Newsletter Earl's Court, Autumn 1978

A free newsletter, printed on thin paper from a Gestetner machine, was now circulating in the immediate area. It was called *Response*, if I recall correctly. Neil Bartlett, an enterprising young writer and social activist who lived in the area, had conceived the idea of a free newspaper that could be written and edited by local unemployed residents.

He offered cheap advertising to local retailers; the newspaper was then effectively printed by hand and distributed to the counters of the local shopkeepers. (A similar idea to the *Big Issue* magazine, really, but preceding it by some years.) Kensington and Chelsea Council were happy to get some recovering addicts and other lost young folk off the streets and working at something that might lead to a job, so they provided minimal funding. When I joined they were working from an old church building. Neil was dark, forceful, energetic and droll, a natural leader. He was said to have had a huge hit with his first play which had been staged when he was 19 or so but, although still full of ideas, had had only very modest success subsequently.

I had become aware of this curious handmade local newspaper because Neil had brought it into the shop and Mother and I happily agreed to display it. With the news of the shop folding – there had been an interview with my mother in *Response* in which she had modified the shop's history to suit herself – Neil suggested that if I now had time I should come over to the office and help with writing and paste-up and whatever else might occur. This seemed a reasonable idea, so I came along.

One of the *quid pro quos* on which *Response* operated was free tickets to new films that were playing at the local art-house cinema. That is, the manager of the Paris Pullman sent us two passes, either to the opening Friday afternoon show at his cinema, or to the trade show for an upcoming film. These were held in a Soho screening room, usually on a Monday morning, and were organised by the film's distributor, for reviewers. (Distributing companies commonly buy the territorial rights for a newly completed film that has been seen at a film festival, then plan an advertising campaign and negotiate a rate with cinema chains which then pay a rental percentage to show the film. Momentum, October, Pathé are examples of recently active distributors.)

I was a notorious film buff (read 'film bore') even then. Neil suggested I might like to go to see the new films and then write reviews for the paper. I was delighted of course. Now my guilty secret of ten years or more could be put to some use. Those 6x4" cards had been a rehearsal for review writing. I had recorded the director, stars, story source, and a short commentary on every film. The cards have long since gone, but the time spent writing them served me as practical training for concise expression. So now I was to write a review that in a small way would actually be published.

In the late 1970s going to the trade shows was always fun. For myself I have always loved to go to the cinema early in the day. The mind is crisper, there is a sense that this is business, not mere indulgent idleness. The screenings held at the big West End cinemas were the most dramatic. They would be hired by distributors to show a new film usually at 10.00am or 10.30am on a Monday morning, three clear hours before the place opened to the general public. The screening was for reviewers from the daily newspapers and weekly magazines, the release date for the film usually being the Friday of that same week. In those days monthly magazine staff writers with longer film star interview pieces, along with the Sunday paper magazine sections, would have been shown the film some ten to twelve weeks previously (their publication requirements meant longer lead times).

On those cold Monday mornings, the grand cinemas in Leicester Square would be closed up, but with one side door open. One of the uniformed doormen, with a trim PR girl in attendance, would be standing just inside the open door. He might give you a grudging nod, she would dimple her hello, and toss her expensive highlights as she checked her clipboard to find your name. Very like being on the guest list for an exclusive club. You would climb the steps up to the designated auditorium. On the other side of the vestibule, you'd often see a Hoover still thrumming, a weary cleaner still in attendance. Another bent back would be polishing the chilled drinks dispenser or re-stuffing the loose popcorn in the vending bins at the sales counter. The great entertainment palace was being readied for the day's imminent public onslaught. But at that early hour, for we select few, there was often a table with real coffee and fresh doughnuts and croissants just outside our auditorium. We would file in. Another PR person would hand us a printed sheet that was a crib: giving the plot set-up but not the whole narrative. The full cast list and the tech crew were always listed, along with the previous hits of the director and principal cast.

As we entered, some of the established journalists would nod at one another but otherwise people rarely spoke. About half had a note pad on their knee. Some had a favoured part of the cinema that they preferred to sit in, others appeared to flop into the first available chair. It was rare for there to be any introductory presentation of any kind – there was, instead, a business-like sense of 'let's get on with it'. The film would come on, the sound often rather bright and hard in an under-populated hall, but the print was always almost fresh from the lab, crisp and clean, with the colours sharp and clear and no projector track marks or damaged splices. Good or bad, in two hours or so the film would come to its eventual end. The lights would come up and we would all stir slowly back into reality. Usually, people said very little as they left the hall.

On the table outside the auditorium the coffee and juice would have been replenished, and wine would now be on offer. Perhaps sandwiches or tasty nibbles. Quite a few people from the PR firm might be there, more occasionally a producer or two and possibly the director of the film. The director was always the unshaved one with the wan smile in an expensively cut but well-worn leather jacket and very creased jeans. He had probably just been collected from the airport an hour before and was on his way to another much more important event on the other side of Europe. Those who dared might speak to him. But the golden rule at this moment was never to comment on the film we had just watched in any but the very vaguest of terms. 'Clean print' you might observe or, 'It must have been nice shooting in Florence' or, 'Was that Debussy they were playing in the café scene?' would be representative remarks. The key, I remember, was not to betray whether you had enjoyed – or disliked – the film in any degree whatever.

The PR people, of course, would be beaming at you and refilling your cup all the while, and asking, 'Pretty wonderful, don't you think?' or 'It's great to see Meryl Streep again, isn't it? Hollywood's pretty sure there's going to be a lot of nominations, don't you agree?' The correct form was to offer something very neutral in reply, polite but unrevealing.

The first couple of times I went to these events I was so over-excited I blurted out something specific about whatever it was that we'd just seen, 'Oh yeah – she's great, I'm sure it'll be huge' or 'Hey, Scorsese is my favourite director, how can you miss?' and then I caught the scornful glares of all the other old hands. I think the notion was that a professional reviewer doesn't want to give too much of a hint because then some influential people will be very hurt if they believe they had been promised a positive response when the actual review turned out to be much more qualified.

Those pre-release screenings were often also staged in small viewing studios in Soho basements. These small viewing theatres were often right next door to famed international restaurants, or infamous strip joints, or the eccentric tailoring shops or musical instrument repairers that were the heart of Soho in those days. Some of the viewing rooms were very posh indeed, some of them depressingly worn and dingy. All of them were 40- or 65-seat halls that could be hired for private events. Review screenings held here would be entirely business-like, with people filing in very promptly and generally leaving immediately when the screening was over, their offices – and lunch – often being very close by. I remember more than once emerging into Wardour Street at the end of a baffling Werner Herzog documentary or some dire Cannon Films euro-thriller with Dolph Lundgren or similar in the lead and wishing I too could go off for a Soho lunch on expenses as some others invariably did. I'd bus it back to Earl's Court and then I'd type up 200 words of rather laboured commentary on whatever masterpiece I'd just sat through and in due time it would appear in *Response*.

The nearest art-house cinema to the *Response*'s offices was the Paris Pullman. It was in a very narrow residential side-street just off the Fulham Road and showed subtitled foreign films almost exclusively. A single hall with about 250 remarkably uncomfortable seats, the sound was tinny, the screen dirty (from nicotine) and the drapes were nearly always tangled. A charming and unique feature of this little hall, one that I have never seen attempted anywhere else, was a little tea-hut in one corner beside the screen. Just before show time, and in any interval in a double bill programme, a pair of little cupboard doors would open up facing into the hall on the right-hand side of the screen, to reveal a small counter, a bubbling urn for tea or coffee, and a small but welcome array of chocolates and cookies. Ice-cream tubs were a possibility also. The Paris Pullman was an undeniably bohemian corner of the cinema firmament, but certainly not without its own eccentric appeal. Nevertheless, if whatever film was screening had been well reviewed – by more august pens than mine – then the films were often well attended and runs of three or four weeks were not uncommon. After all, Channel Four had yet to appear on our TV screens and we were still a year or so away from the beginning of the first full wave of domestic VHS or Betamax videotape players.

I was forever going over to the Paris Pullman either to drop off copies of *Response* or to see the Friday early afternoon screening of the new film if no preview tickets had been arranged. The manager of the Pullman was a bulky, good natured, very pale man of middle years who was thickening fast as he never exercised. Jeff was fond of a beer, but never to excess that I saw. He tended to sweat, and he lived in a windowless cubbyhole of an office that was actually behind the cinema screen itself. This could make conversation difficult at times. If a film were nearing its climax, a car chase or a hysterical door-slamming family row by shouting and subtitled Italians perhaps, we would be obliged to stand chest-to-chest bellowing to each other over the scream of tyres or the voluble weeping of the hero.

I liked Jeff, and he was amused by my rather misplaced enthusiasm for films. Cinema managers are involved in a specialised form of retailing: they care only that their seats be ready, then full, then tidied, then refilled with fresh customers three or four times a day. If a given film causes this to happen more readily than another then it is demonstrably a good film. That's it. My enthusiastic chatter about narrative patterns and star personae and mise-en-scène was utterly beside the point to Jeff, but he was very avuncular, nevertheless.

Jeff was employed by Contemporary Films which operated the Paris Pullman cinema. Contemporary Films was owned by Charles and Kitty Cooper with James Quinn as a minority partner. In the 1950s Quinn had been instrumental in helping to set up the British Film Institute and its cinema, the National Film Theatre, based at the South Bank. He was now retired but had an investment interest in the Paris Pullman. He had experimented with running late-night film shows, which were proving to be quite successful. These were screenings of older feature films that began at eleven at night, so finishing at 1.00am or significantly later on Fridays and Saturdays when he would book double bills which would finish close to 3.00am.

This sort of scheduling can be very tiring for cinema staff. Cinema working is a notoriously underpaid line of work, even now. When the legal minimum wage became law in the 1990s it was a death knell for quite a lot of the older halls as they had historically been paying well below any notional minimum wage, probably since the era of silent films.

The Paris Pullman, Chelsea pre 1971

Opened in 1911, this cinema was originally known as Bolton's Picture Playhouse. It became a live theatre after the Second World War. In November 1955, the façade was reconstructed, and it re-opened as the Paris Pullman. It closed in 1983 and was demolished; a block of flats now occupies the site.

Cinema Theatre Association Archive

The Paris Pullman, Chelsea Winter 1978

Jeff was not happy at having to work the extended hours these late shows required. His assistant manager had refused outright to work them, not even the modest pay enhancement would entice him and having threatened to resign, he did. Jeff was now in rather a quandary and amazed me utterly by asking me to consider becoming his new assistant manager.

I was simultaneously dumbfounded and delighted. James Quinn now asked to meet me and had suggested that I might also take over the responsibility for the late-night shows and also programme the films for each month. From my point of view, I would get to choose whatever films I liked from whatever was available to rent and show them in whatever single- or double-bill I liked. He agreed he would cover the cost of programme notes for each month's scheduling cycle which I intended to model on the programme hand-outs that the BFI National Film Theatres at the South Bank gave out at most screenings. I was dazed with the possibilities ahead.

As I left his front door, I shook his hand and suddenly thought to ask,

'How much are you going to pay me, Mr Quinn?'

'Ah, I thought £40 a week?' he replied evenly.

'Thank you, again,' I said beaming away.

What Mr Quinn didn't know was that I had been on £11.50 a week dole money for eight months since the closure of Dad's bookshop so his offer of an income of £40 a week sounded like more riches than I could spend in a lifetime.

The staff at the Pullman were a very mixed lot. There was a constant trickle of student travellers who were looking for pin-money to keep them financially afloat while they visited London. They were often tanned Australians or New Zealanders, Earl's Court being then, as now, an area saturated with cheap long- and short-stay hostels: indeed, the area was known back then as 'Kangaroo Valley' and was said to be a notoriously easy area for crashing a lively party or two on any weekend night. The students who worked at the Pullman always had names like Kiki or Jake and were so relaxed they were almost horizontal.

The more permanent staff included Mrs Griggs, a sour Scots woman in a ginger wig, who occupied the cash desk three evenings a week, glared angrily at all the patrons, and whose cash tin always balanced to the penny any night she sat in the booth, no matter how busy we had been. Another was a woman from East Germany called Anna-Lise. Anna-Lise was north of fifty years of age, wraith thin, with high cheekbones and badly dyed hair that changed colour almost with her mood. She wore bangles and festoons of beads and chipped nail varnish which always matched at least two of the several colours she would wear at any one time. She spoke the most wonderful, fractured English of her own devising: 'Vunderful film, Herr Nick, but disgustful in zer bedroom scenes. Zer French are perverts film-peeples, are zey not?' she would say after sitting at the back through some new romance by François Truffaut or Claude Lelouch. I suspected her of being one of those quiet old-style Earl's Court junkies who was getting a regular legal fix on the National Health as a registered user. She had lived in Britain for quite some years, having escaped from the DDR via Hungary at the end of the 1950s. She was given to alarming mood swings at times, beginning the evening in a very cheery mood when she came on duty at 9.00pm to do the last evening house followed by the late show. 'Ah, gutt hevening Herr Nick, you are vurry well, I am hoping. But no, you are coughing much, hiss bad to cough so much, medicine you have? Und a gutt ducktor?'

She would then settle into the tea-hutch and hand out paper cups to grateful customers for fifteen minutes at the start of the evening's late show. But then, on occasion, after an hour or two, I would find her at the back of the hall, wringing her hands and weeping copious silent tears 'Ah, Herr Nick, I ham unvell again. Hit hiss mine nervousness, you know. I am vishing to go home, high haplogise but hit is vurry necessary for me...' This didn't happen often enough to justify dismissing Anna-Lise, but it could leave us inconveniently short in a rush. And Jeff felt a loyalty to Anna-Lise. She had, apparently, been working at the cinema so long that he saw her as almost part of the fixtures. We both felt sorry for her in a way that we never did for other unreliable members of the crew.

Life at the Paris Pullman continued for about a year or so. Jeff and I worked a strict two-days-on, two-days-off cycle. Work started at about 11.00am and finished about 1.00am Sunday to Thursday, with Fridays and Saturdays ending close to 3.00am. Years later I met a retired manager of the old school who averred that cinema managers invariably took on the job because they abhorred early starts. It is true that I never kept the hours of a baker or a postman, but even with its mid-morning start the hours of cinema work always ran very late. They also tended to cut into one's own leisure in the sense that getting time off for a whole weekend or a special family occasion, like a wedding perhaps, would always take extensive forward timetabling and permission seeking. A cinema manager is perforce committed to entertaining the public during their own leisure hours.

At eleven each morning you would unlock the service side door to let yourself in, switch off the security alarm system and check that the night cleaners had done a proper job: hall, seats, vestibule carpet, toilets, glass doors, etc. You would note any failed light bulbs in the public areas to report later to the projectionists. (A convention existed, in those days at least, that the projectionist and his team were responsible to the manager for maintenance of all the house lighting.) Bulbs would be replaced immediately if they were over exits or other safety areas. About once a fortnight there would be a 'lamping-up' session when all the other dud bulbs would be replaced. As duty manager you were on hand to supervise deliveries and attend to planned or unplanned site visits. And there was always plenty of paperwork to fill up the quiet times. About 12.30pm the day staff would come on to prepare the kiosk and set up the cash box for sales.

This was still the era of automat numbered paper tickets on a narrow, perforated roll, quite unlike the digitised systems of today. The ticket rolls would have different colours, for matinees, or OAPs, or children, or full price, whatever. The senior doorman, or the most reliable of the occasional staff, would be sent round to unchain all the emergency exits. These chains were then delivered to the manager's office where there would be a specific chain rack to receive them. The chains, when off the doors, had to be placed so they were readily in view of the duty manager's desk at all times. There was, and probably still is, a standing safety regulation that such a procedure be maintained in all London cinemas. At 1.00pm or close to it the staff would open the doors for the first house of the day.

There are some people who only attend films early on weekday afternoons. They are often, but by no means always, elderly.

They are almost always shabby of aspect and grey of pallor. They attend alone, sit apart, rarely smile or laugh at whatever they see on the screen. In the more extreme cases they seem to be entirely indifferent to the film – the cinema is simply a destination. They sometimes return the following Monday at the same time and sit through the same film without comment. (Tuesday the library, Wednesday the clinic, Thursday the bingo, Friday the post office: you get the idea.) Sad, really. The early part of the week was almost always quiet, with even the evening houses not filling more than half. Sometimes the cinema owners would decide to promote half price tickets on a Monday to cheer up trade a bit. This usually had the effect of killing Tuesdays stone dead, but it was, and still is, a popular move with the public, so most cinemas have some version of this, even today.

The weekends are naturally livelier. The new films almost always open on a Friday, in all halls. The reviews will appear on Thursday or Friday as a general rule, so as to promote the new film as much as possible from the start. How exactly a film begins to build the vital 'good word of mouth' is something that distributors (and indeed the studios) have been trying to calculate since they were first created over a hundred years ago. Some films are infamous in the trade for having been the beneficiaries of huge promotional campaigns, cast with established stars, only to open to yawning voids in all halls and be withdrawn after two weeks, never to be heard of again – save perhaps fifteen years later as the filler title on a Johnny Depp or Sylvester Stallone four film box set. Equally there are films entirely cast with unknowns that have a huge following from their very first screenings and build to unstoppable tides of repeat business, so that everyone connected with them makes a sizable fortune.

A legendary example of this is, believe it or not, *Star Wars*, the very first instalment in that now long-established multi-film cycle. The first film was cast with unknowns (save Alec Guinness in a small but plot-significant role, and he was not really a star in America) and with a narrative set to the conventions of old-school sci-fi, a genre that had almost never been known to bring big profits to a producer or prestige to a studio. Twentieth Century Fox had frankly very modest expectations of a film that was predicted to attract only a very specialised potential audience. Yet, as Hollywood history recalls, George Lucas' labour of love, with its modest advertising and a plot and dramatic style based on the Saturday morning cinema serials of the 1940s and 50s (a cinematic form consigned to film history three decades earlier), had queues stretching around the cinemas from its opening morning. Even after several promising test screenings in California, few people, save George Lucas himself perhaps, had any prodigious expectations of what *Star Wars* might eventually become. And yet, as he reported many years later of that memorable opening weekend, 'How did they know, man?'

At the Pullman, weekend evenings were always busy. This meant that the weekend evening shows at least needed careful seating of patrons as well as enough staff to do the seating and the subsequent clearing out for the late-night, double-feature show that would begin soon after. Not absolutely taxing, but a set of tasks that required planning, an established routine for staff procedure and enough flexibility to allow for the unexpected.

For example, I learned in time to always carry a small screwdriver in my evening waistcoat pocket. One or other of the Pullman's worn old seats was apt to fail on its bracket just as we were seating a capacity house. I would have to dive into the row, push past dozens of knees, get down on the dusty floor, often with an aggrieved patron standing directly above me whose candid public commentary on the shortcomings of the cinema, the chair, and the ice-cream now melting in his hand in general would soon pass to the more specific shortcomings of my own parentage and the state of my hair as an index of all the world's current failings. All this as I wrestled the damaged chair back into its supporting bracket and screwed it in tight. All the while, trying to apologise blithely to the unimpressed pair of shoes under my nose. Such adventures always delay the start of the film which can lead to a further set of complications if one is not prompt in action. All this fun every weekend night and not forgetting the magnificent £40 a week in wages.

About once a week I would be required to go to the Paris Pullman's head office in Soho to take up formal records of ticket returns or ancillary sales (the ice-creams, the coffees and the paper cups they were dispensed in, etc, etc) or staff changes and new employments. I always enjoyed these visits. Contemporary Films had an office on Wardour Street above a shop supplying film camera and lenses and lights for purchase or rental. This shop space had once been part of the display entrance to the firm itself, but rising rents meant the owners, Charles and Kitty Cooper, had now sub-let the ground floor shop space to this nominally separate film equipment rental firm.

Up the rickety stairs to the first floor there was a grubby warren of small offices, all of them with two telephones each, most of which rang incessantly. Actually, they blurred into a sort of muffled purr whenever they demanded attention. To have had them ring with the conventional clatter would have been intolerable. Contemporary Films had been in business some decades and the Coopers were well known in the very specialist world of cinema and film trading. Like a street full of jewellers or doctors, the firms along Wardour Street were all linked professionally, each supplying some part of the film-making equation to the others, each united by ancient alliances and divided by even more ancient feuds and border-wars that permeated all their relationships. Contemporary Films was seen as a small firm of longevity and modest historical distinction (i.e., some few of the films they had distributed in the past had sold memorably impressive numbers of tickets) and Charles and Kitty Cooper were seen as canny old traders, albeit rather past their heyday now, and less and less given to risk-taking with the newly minted films they took on at international film festivals to promote and rent out. Nevertheless, the films they did choose often made a respectable return, and were, as often as not, burnished by respectful reviews from the broadsheets.

Charles Cooper always wore a suit, a suit that had been very well made long ago and now needed altering to fit his slightly shrunken frame. He did all the PR and glad-handing of promoters and directors and senior journalists who passed through the office. Very occasionally there would be some sort of public launch of a new title and Charles was always present at these events wearing a very professional smile. Kitty kept the books. She was a dried grey prune of a woman, a very hard worker who knew her trade well and absolutely lacked any trace of levity. Yet she commanded loyalty – there were two or three among the fifteen or so who worked in that warren who had been with Contemporary since the firm's outset.

One Friday I was up at the office on my routine visit with the paperwork when I was asked to go to Kitty's office. This summons was not absolutely new, but it wasn't common either. I went along the corridor feeling suddenly rather unsettled. I knocked and then pushed at the open chipboard door. The office reminded me of Raskolnikov's grim room, every surface was piled with papers, dingy plans and charts hung on the walls, some newer crisper ones pinned up over the older ones. She was seated and grunting argumentatively into a telephone. She looked up, gave a smile as thin as a razor and gestured towards a seat that was piled with papers also. She waved to indicate that I should move them somewhere, anywhere. She turned back to the phone:

'No, Edward, you know that's too much. Five per cent is quite enough. No, Edward, no!' She was hissing with apparent fury now. 'Never. How many years have we been doing this? Look darling, someone's just come in. I've got to see to this. Can I call you back in fifteen? Right, thanks sweetie, bye.'

The switch in her voice was startling. My slight anxiety at this unexpected summons was now compounded. Kitty looked at me quite carefully. Then she said without any preamble,

'How would you like to go to Oxford? The assistant manager there is leaving and Barry, the manager, needs someone to start on Monday week. How much are we paying you now?'

'£40 a week,' I replied too off-balance to think or calculate.

'Right, £50, then.' Her mouth was a straight grey line.

'To be assistant manager at the cinema in Oxford?' I asked, trying to be clear about what was happening.

'Yes, yes – you went to Oxford, didn't you?' she barked. 'No,' I replied, 'I've never been there except once to visit a friend and to go to the theatre. Where would I stay?'

This did give her pause for a moment, she seemed not to have thought of it. Then she said,

'I know – the lad who's leaving. You could take over his place, couldn't you?' This was sounding risky to me now.

'I need time to think it over,' I demurred.

'Monday at ten then – I need to settle this immediately,' Kitty replied, looking at me accusingly.

She grabbed up the phone and waved me away. I turned and left, half excited, half furious. It's never very gratifying to be reminded just how exactly one is seen simply as an employee by one's employer.

That weekend both at home and at work at the Pullman I

kept chewing it over. Spending the rest of my working life in Jeff's smoky cubbyhole behind the Paris Pullman's screen wasn't the summit of my life's ambition, even with the creative leavening within the job that was programming the late shows. Oxford might be a challenge – it was, perhaps, gratifying to be asked to take the post at least. Jeff was non-committal about whether he thought it would be a step up for me to go. He didn't dismiss the idea, but he wasn't enthusiastic about it either. From his point of view if I left he'd have to train someone up and there was no guarantee that whoever that person was would achieve the tasks he would set them even to my pitifully moderate standard.

I was really perplexed. I didn't want to leave London with all my friends and family and the cinemas that I visited three or four times a week. I had a life that suited me in the big city – indeed my life had been markedly more enjoyable with the security of a steady job. I was living at home in my old childhood room, paying a very nominal rent to my mother. We saw very little of each other. I slept late and she wrote in her study much of the time. Everything was in balance. And yet, and yet. I was 27 and didn't need to be stuck in a post education rut forever. After all, Oxford was not very far away, and my mother had known the university in her own student days and had fond memories of her time there. Perhaps it was worth the risk.

On the Monday morning I called Kitty at 10.05am and said that I had decided to take the opportunity.

'Fine,' she grunted, 'I'll ring Barry and tell him you're starting next week. Thanks.'

She hung up. I wondered how high was the cliff that I had just agreed to jump off with such scant ceremony. I was reminded of the man who leaps off a hundred storey building. As he passes the ninetieth floor he says, to encourage himself, 'So far, so good'; as he passes the fiftieth floor he is heard to say, 'Okay so far'; as he passes the twentieth floor he says, 'Seems okay up to now…'

The Phoenix, Oxford, 1995
The North Oxford Kinema, as it was originally called, opened in 1913 and was designed by local architect Gilbert T Gardiner. In 1920 it was renamed the Scala and in 1930 sound equipment was installed. The auditorium was divided to make two screens in 1970. Over the years it became one of the most important art-house cinemas in the United Kingdom outside London. New owners gave it the name The Phoenix in 1977 and in 1989 it became the first cinema in what became the Picturehouse brand.

Malcolm Graham (POX0028423:2008.8.1644) Oxfordshire County Council Oxfordshire History Centre – www.pictureoxon.org.uk

The Phoenix Cinema, Oxford
Summer 1979

There was no time to lose so I decided I would go to Oxford immediately. I rang Jeff at the Pullman and asked him for the phone number of the Phoenix Cinema in Oxford.

'So you're going, then?' he said.

He didn't sound surprised. He gave me the number and, ringing it directly, I had a small stroke of luck. The soon-to-be-outgoing assistant manager answered the phone. He agreed to see me immediately and to take me and show me where he was staying in Oxford. I said I would be there later that afternoon and would stay the night if that could be managed. He thought something could be arranged.

I threw a very few items into a hold-all and set straight off to the coach terminus near Victoria station. There was a non-stop bus to Oxford from Victoria Coach station every hour in those days. In ninety minutes I was in 'the city of dreaming spires'. I found my way to Walton Street and so to the Phoenix cinema. The Phoenix had a small frontage and two screens. The larger hall seated approximately 180 and the other more like 60. It was an attractively shabby little art-house that, in 1979, concentrated on the likes of Fassbinder and Herzog and Chabrol and Olmi, with the occasional revival of a British period Hitchcock or a Buster Keaton comedy or a similar title. The assistant manager was Kevin. He was certainly no older than I, slight, wearing a far from clean white shirt and rayon tie.

He had a lot of gel in his black hair. When he smiled he revealed dozens of small grey teeth. He shook hands, a single greasy tug, and invited me up to the office.

Another clapboard lined cubbyhole, this time at the top of a flight of stairs, but with a single dirty window that gave a good view of the pair of black wheelie bins out in the small brick yard. Kevin proceeded to show me all the basic elements of administrative housekeeping and the safe combination and similar quotidian elements of the operation.

After an hour or so we went downstairs to meet the staff. I was presented with a very standard group of folk that are usual for a provincial house. They were older ladies and young mums in the main: people for whom the adaptable hours of the job and the lack of need for any very continuous exertion were compensation enough for the low wages. Compared to being a waitress, being a cinema usherette is very rarely physically taxing, it requires very little English and is indoors and in the warm. If both the commute and the manager are tolerable then it can make a good second job for someone who already does night cleaning or hospital portering, or someone who just wants to supplement her household's very meagre income.

Mrs Harris was the uncontested doyenne of the Phoenix Cinema's staff. She had been in post at the Phoenix for many years, indeed she had been there before it had arisen from the ashes of its previous avatar, the Gaumont. She nursed an unrequited passion for Leslie Howard and held command of the sales kiosk, the key to which she guarded most carefully beneath her spreading skirts. She was clear-eyed, wore old-fashioned powder on her face and a mouth always pursed to disapprove of all that was novel or irregular, yet within her frame of reference she was entirely competent and accurate. The other two ladies and young Cheryl, in her tight sweaters and boots, all deferred to her comfortably enough. I would guess that Mrs H had never accepted a position as assistant manager because she had everything exactly where she wanted it and, anyway, she viewed 'managing' as a man's job.

It was here at the Phoenix that I soon decided to grow the beard that I have worn all my life since. By the second week I was in post I had become a little self-conscious of being so fresh faced and of ordering all these older ladies to their positions as the cycle of each day moved along. In those days I was a very slight 27-year-old, an alien to the town, and conscious that I needed to be able to present at least a convincing illusion of authority to the public just as much as to the staff. The beard, when it first appeared, was rather sparse, more reminiscent of five-a-side football. But in time it thickened and established itself as a slightly darker shade than the brown hair on my head – and I liked the freedom of not having to shave on a daily basis.

On the day of my arrival, Barry, the general manager, though on duty, was still at lunch apparently, so I was to meet him later. I reminded Kevin that I had nowhere to live in Oxford and that accordingly I would be interested in seeing the room he would be vacating very soon. He agreed and I said that I'd go for a stroll about the town and return to meet him at six when he finished his shift. So, I walked out into the street, blinking in the pale sunlight. I felt quite encouraged really. The job was the same but not absolutely so. The people outside looked recognisably like the denizens of London. The narrow streets, some still cobbled, were a novelty; the sandstone walls glowed with a quiet permanence that was vastly soothing. In the broader streets there were bustle and familiar brand names. There were bicycling undergraduates and grannies with baskets and tourists with maps. Not far away I discovered a rival cinema. This was the Odeon in George Street

– three screens showing all the mainstream Hollywood fare, a double bill of *Grease* with *Saturday Night Fever* was typical here, so their programming was not really any threat to us.

And then I discovered Blackwell's, the cathedral of all bookshops. Blackwell's actually has a number of sites in Oxford these days, but back then it lay at the end of Broad Street, supplying the town with all the latest novels and the university with texts and commentaries of every degree of complexity and giddying erudition. The main building is still a warren of small landings and corridors and small and large rooms rammed with literature in all the languages known to man. At the back of the ground floor, I discovered a magical landing. This leads down to a huge basement area called 'The Norrington Room'. This vast sales area of shelf upon shelf upon shelf contained, it seemed to me, all that life's future reading could ever desire… If the proverbial infinite number of monkeys had the proverbial infinite amount of time they would be better employed here than trying to type up the plays of Shakespeare by sheer mathematical happenstance. They might spend their infinite time reading this infinity of books and thus becoming in time excellent university graduates by sheer application. I was to spend hours and hours in Blackwell's in the coming months, choosing and tasting and comparing writers.

The shop became my solace, my library, my refuge, almost a home.

At 5.55pm precisely I returned to the cinema to meet up with Kevin. He had taken off his tie and was wearing a green and blue tracksuit top. We got on a bus and rode about nine or ten stops southwards. 'I'll cook for us tonight,' he volunteered. I was impressed and pleased.

'That's nice. Great idea – shall I get some wine?' He shot me a look. 'Or beer perhaps?'

'Yeah, couple of cans, yeah? I'll show you where.'

We got off the bus. I had the idea that we were somewhere near the outskirts of Abingdon. The streets were domestic. Terraced rows, corner shops, a laundrette, very ordinary. At the bus stop was a corner shop with an exhausted looking woman in a sari behind the till. I bought four cans of beer. We walked the length of a street and turned a corner into another shabby terrace. The light was fading.

'Here we are,' said Kevin, stopping suddenly and stepping through a low open gate and across a scrap of utterly neglected front garden and mounting some steps up to a black front door.

His key opened the door into a hallway that displayed only a worn sisal runner, a well-used child's pushchair and a rather dented bicycle. He turned the knob of the very first door he came to saying, 'Here we are,' again. I followed him into the front room. It was the classic bed-sit, all too familiar from my own student days of only a year or two back.

There was a rumpled single bed against the far wall, a bow window with a view of the broken little gate we had just come through, a largish table behind the door against the wall opposite the bed. There were two unmatched straight chairs pushed against the table. On the table was a very small television, a cruet of stamped grey metal and bottles of condiments. The carpet was fitted throughout and had once been a burgundy colour but was now a grey impasto of grime and wear. There was a neon strip for a ceiling light and one shaded lamp on a rickety stool next to the bed. The two floor length curtains that framed the window were patterned and faded and hung crookedly.

'Loo and bath are at the back. Not bad for £22.75 a week, plus bills of course, huh? Back in a moment.'

He turned away, throwing his tracksuit top over one of the chairs as he left the room.

I stood alone in the middle of this sad, sad little room and thought to myself that I couldn't live here unless I was utterly desperate. To be away from home in a strange town where I knew no one and trying to do a job that suddenly seemed rather daunting – after all, I had only nodded at the staff and now I realised with a slightly anxious thrill of surprise that I hadn't even met the manager, with whom I would be working closely. 'And to give up half my pittance to pay for this rat-hole,' I thought very sourly. It was a very sobering moment for me. To think of all the people who lived in rooms little better than this, or not even as nice. People who worked all their lives as disposable employees and so always lived in rented rooms. I winced when I thought of the privileges that I had taken for granted.

Kevin came back in and smiling said,

'But you haven't taken your coat off!'

I grinned apologetically and hung my coat over the other chair. Kevin now opened a fitted wardrobe door that I hadn't noticed. There were shelves and a hanging space on one side and, set into the other, a small metal kitchen sink and taps, a Belling electric oven with two small hot plates on the top, and a couple of shelves built into the inside of the wardrobe door for dry goods. There was a short row of cooking tools above the shelves and a small caravan fridge on the floor to the side of the sink. It was all rather neat, in fact, and had been very well fitted together, if not very recently. My heart rose slightly at the sight of this evidence of order and planning and convenient organisation. Kevin began to bustle about opening tins and putting pans on to boil.

'I can borrow a mattress for you from Cheryl upstairs later,' he said. 'You remember her, from the cinema…? With the boots?' he prompted.

Then I remembered her from the very brief meeting with the staff earlier that afternoon.

'She's upstairs – got a kid, and her bloke's in the Army – Northern Ireland she says, but they're not married, Mrs H says.'

I thought to myself that Mrs H would be the sort who would at least think she knew all the staff's secrets, especially if they could be construed as discreditable.

In not too long a time Kevin produced spaghetti and tinned tomatoes and sliced grilled peppers and a chipped saucer each with green lettuce leaves and carrot shavings upon them. He offered a bottle of salad cream. It was plain but perfectly decent, and decently offered. I opened two of the beer cans. He chatted rather vaguely about the cinema. I asked about Barry Stephens, the manager. Kevin looked a bit guarded – then said,

'Well, you may as well know, cos you'll find it out for yourself soon enough; he's a drunk. Not too bad in the mornings if he's not hung over, but by the afternoon he can be pretty far gone. Often spends the weekday evenings in the boozer across the road once the house has gone in. Can be a right pain. He's not always like that mind, but it does get you down at times.'

I looked at him.

'So that's why you're moving on?'

Kevin looked a bit sheepish.

'Well, I've got a slot in a new hall in Chipping Ongar – three screens, £70 a week and half of one per cent of sales. Wouldn't you?'

At last, I saw what I had walked into – and all for not asking the right questions. Ah, the guilelessness of youth. Kitty Cooper had played a very deft hand. Kevin was leaving. She and Charles needed an assistant to a manager who was himself semi-functional at best. In fact, they were in urgent need of a combined minder and nursemaid and administrative stooge. I wasn't very thrilled. We finished our meal together rather quietly.

I offered to wash up but Kevin suggested that if I dried that would be enough. I wiped the damp plates and crocks he handed me with a piece of grey towel and placed them back on the table. By the time I had finished he had turned off the taps and wiped down the little sink. He knelt and pulled two medium-sized cardboard boxes out from under the table we had been sitting at.

'These go in here,' he said and slipped the plates neatly into one box and the cutlery and other items into the other. He pushed the two boxes back with a practised foot. 'Right! Telly or pub?' he asked. I said,

'Telly's cheaper – and we've still got two cans.'

'Good enough,' Kevin said, giving me an appreciative grin.

I was pleased I'd made the choice I had. In truth I'd no yen for an evening in a smoky boozer, and I guessed that Kevin probably spent his money cautiously, and so felt ashamed again of my view of his clothes and his appearance earlier in the day.

After two hours or so Kevin went upstairs to fetch the mattress. When he brought it down it turned out to be two large, padded cushions that might have been part of a sofa once. They had once been beige but were now stained and well worn. Kevin pulled two nylon sheets and a thin blanket from his wardrobe and handed them to me.

'Hope these'll do,' he said. He was embarrassed and so was I, my sense of imminent discomfort perhaps more obvious than I thought.

'No worries,' I said. 'I'll use the bathroom first, shall I?'

Something of our mutual embarrassment was born also of being two blokes now feeling the slight lack of privacy. In the event we were both under our separate covers in ten minutes. It was not a good night for me. I lay there thinking of the long day with very mixed feelings of how I had been bamboozled into taking this slot at a new cinema and the thought that I would have to make a serious effort to find somewhere else to live that would be both tolerable and affordable.

This I knew would not be easy. Oxford is a university city and the colleges have many more students and dons and other staff than they can accommodate, so affordable rooms for rent anywhere near the centre of town have always been at a premium since at least the middle of the 19th century. In the event I was to inherit Kevin's room for a week after he moved out while I looked for somewhere that wasn't so depressing. By the end of that week, I had found a largish upper room in a newly built house on a brand-new housing estate outside Oxford. This was at Charlgrove which was twelve full miles southeast of the town and so a rather lengthy bus ride to and from my bed to my desk. But that bedroom was bright and cheery, the house and its common parts fairly clean and the other mortgage tenant (someone to rent the spare bedroom and so help to pay the monthly charge) seemed pleasant enough.

When I met him at 10.30am on that first Monday morning neither Barry Stephens nor I were impressed with each other. He saw, I suspect, a tousled and be-spectacled short arse with too young a face and a suspiciously posh London accent while I saw a man in early middle years already badly gone to fat, in a filthy rumpled shirt and greasy tangled tie who had yellow teeth and an urgent need of a haircut. He stuck out a meaty hand that had a good growth of hair on the back.

'Morning,' he said shortly. 'You'd better come upstairs.'

The same upstairs office of last week seemed rather smaller

today. There were timesheets and stock records and wages calculation ready-reckoners all in a heap on top of the desk.

'You know about this stuff, I suppose?' he grunted doubtfully.

Suddenly I was glad that Kevin and I had had that hour together the previous week.

'I did stock and ticket reconciliations with the manager at the Pullman,' I replied, 'but I haven't really done wages from scratch.'

Barry snorted.

'Well, I'll have to bloody teach you then, won't I?' he snorted again, turning away.

As he turned towards the door he began to cough, a nasty phlegm-sodden wet cough, deep in his chest. He held the door frame a moment, to steady himself. Then he took a cigarette box from his pocket, and pulled one out, none too steadily. He jerked the packet a half inch towards me. I shook my head. He raised one eyebrow very slightly, pushed the cigarette between his wet lips, and lit it with a disposable lighter.

'Helps you breathe.' He coughed gratefully. 'I'm going to unlock, you'd better have a walk round with me,' he finished and turned towards the door.

I spent the rest of the day shadowing Barry, learning the specific arrangements at the Phoenix. Business seemed steady, if not remarkable. As Kevin had hinted, Barry tended to leave the premises for long periods. These were usually during the quieter hours of the trading day, and any weekday evening after the final house had gone in. He would simply take the bulk of the banknotes out of the till, count them very quickly, and then thrust them into a cloth bag, lumber up the stairs and throw the bag onto the floor of the safe and slam the safe door shut. We would not see him again often. He would cross the road to the Red Lion and remain there until either we closed or they did. In one sense it certainly wasn't a bad arrangement. Barry was always in the same bar in the same pub, often on the same seat. If we needed him we knew just where to find him. The problem was he was nearly always very drunk and so unable to make any sensible contribution to whatever crisis had occurred at the cinema. If ever I did decide to advise him of a flooded toilet or an urgent call from head office or a very angry patron who was demanding to see him, Barry would lurch off his stool and stand swaying.

'Wassir matter, need th' keysss? W'as hup, young Nick?' he would slur, grinning, as he looked round to see if anyone was as amused as he was trying to be.

Nobody ever was. I quickly saw that introducing this befuddlement into whatever situation I was trying to handle, back across the road at the cinema, was only likely to worsen things.

We were soon not working shifts together any more than was unavoidable. My disapproval must have been evident, though I never dared say anything direct. In fact, I didn't want to work with Barry if I could avoid it. It was less likely to lead to clashes between us, Mrs Harris could manage him in most public situations, and I detested starting a piece of administrative work, a staff roster for the upcoming two months, perhaps, then being called away downstairs to help with something, only returning to find him slumped in the office chair, a cigarette polluting the air and his whisky glass making damp rings all over my paperwork. Poor Barry, he was a pathetic figure really: unshaven, dirty and really very ill. But he was bellicose, noisy and dismissive of me.

I worked a little over a year in Oxford, making the long commute back and forth to Charlgrove each day I worked. The bus on which I depended seemed a rare beast at the best of times and on Sundays so infrequent as to be almost a news item when it did finally appear.

Then, too, there were the late shows. On Friday and Saturday evenings we would show a final screening of each of our main features beginning at 11.00pm. Separating the public from their money took longer than in the earlier parts of the day because half the audience had already spent some of the evening drinking. Often, they turned up with half-eaten take-aways raising fumes and dripping fat. About 11.30pm I would declare the house full, send all but one usherette home, collect up the floats and the takings from the sales and the ticket kiosks, lock them up, push shut the front doors and turn off the outside sign. This was intended to indicate to any (very) late-comers that they were now seriously late and thus there was little point in their seeking admission. I would retreat upstairs to the office, do the cash up and make the banking record, then put the cash in a bank wallet ready to drop it into the local bank's night safe. We were not insured to have the takings in our safe overnight and so the manager's last duty was always to drop the cash in the night safe after he had locked up for the night. (Even back in the 1980s when I worked at a popular four screen house in Chelsea it was not uncommon to bank three or four thousand pounds in cash several times throughout the course of a busy Saturday.)

The late programme (which here was simply the main feature of the week, just played through one more time) would usually end about 1.30am in the morning. Out into the night would now lurch our slightly sobered patrons to stiffly walk back to their colleges or to find their bicycles, wherever they had contrived to leave them. I would flick on the pair of naked 150 watt 'cleaner's lights' in each hall and walk round each once to check for insensibles or smouldering cigarettes or any significant new damage – broken chairs, tears in the carpeting, exit signs with a failed bulb behind them, that kind of thing. Next the chains were put on the exit doors. In the darkened vestibule I would bid the projectionist and the usherette a brisk goodnight, and chain and lock all the front doors. Then it was a quick nip up to the office, grab my hat and coat and the night's takings from the safe, lock the safe, prime the burglar alarm, and nip down the stairs again. Out the discreet pass door, snapping it shut behind me and checking that the red blink of the alarm had settled to green and then faded away. I now had a short two hundred yards walk to the local bank's night safe, a quick glance round, put the tiny key into the lock, pull the night safe door open, drop the cash wallet in, slam it shut, quick twist of the key and out and into my pocket. Now I was done for the day.

I always aspired to get the cashing up done before the film was over and so be free to nip along to the bank well before final lock-up. I achieved this as often as not, but if there was a discrepancy I would have to search through the figures and the cash until I found it. Being at the end of a day that had started at 10.30am as often as not, this was often taxing work. (Barry of course never bothered with any of this – he would do the reconciliation the next morning. On more than one occasion when he had rung me to invite me to cover for him, I came in to find the cash actually still all over the desk and the safe open, if behind the locked and alarmed office door.)

On weekday evenings I could usually catch the last bus home. But at 1.30am on a weekend night there were definitely no buses to carry me the twelve miles home to my bed. Accordingly, I routinely booked myself a mini-cab to meet me at the front of the cinema and I would doze in a well-used Ford Cortina the 15 minutes back to Charlgrove. With tip this was usually about £3.50.

Once I was indoors it was usually close to 2.00am. Being a weekend occasionally one of my three housemates might be up still making a final cup of tea before bed, but only rarely. Most often I was tired and alone and still slightly running on adrenaline from the stresses of the long day. Very quietly I would make myself a cup in the kitchen at the back of the house. I would open a tin of soup if I felt adventurous enough. Then it was time to creep upstairs, listening to the noises of the sleeping house, and into my room. I had plenty of books and my stereo which I had brought from London. I often listened to a little blues music, to Robert Johnson or Sun House or Mississippi Fred McDowell perhaps, for an hour or so, through the headphones, as I wound down for bed. I think I wanted this time to myself so that I didn't feel too enslaved to the job – that I had some other recourse than simply to fall on my bed in my clothes from sheer exhaustion.

Days off were a bit of a problem at first. Barry and I worked a 'two days on, two days off' rota system at the Phoenix, which was pretty tolerable in theory because this allowed both Barry and me to earn a little overtime every week and to plan our days ahead. But Barry became increasingly inclined, as the months passed, to ring me with some excuse asking me to go in and do a half day for him 'because I've had a bad night and need to go to the doctor' or 'because I've got to wait in for the plumber' or similar. I soon realised that if I was in London on my day off it would be harder for him to do this. However, I was in a dormitory village sixty miles from the metropolis without a car, too far to get there and back by public transport in a day without getting up so early that it would obviate much of the leisure of a free day. Also, I had really no place to stay in the big city. Here I had an enormous stroke of luck.

Apart from cinemas, my favourite haunts have always been record shops and book shops. On the Fulham Road, a hundred yards up from a five-screen cinema, was an independent record shop – long since gone – called 'Raven Records'. I remember it had a cheery bright green theme to its colour scheme, and a green frame to the glass door. There were carpet tiles in three shades of grass green on the floor. There were lovely custom-made wooden display racks for the record albums, and above them wide pin-boards. There was a raised sales counter on the left as you entered, and then the green record bins all round. The display boards were above the record bins, at head height, to display the posters that record companies supplied to retailers in those days, promoting the new and up coming releases. These were still the days of vinyl, of course, with Philips music-cassettes being the only common alternative. The shop window display was often an elaborate promotional sculpture of posters stapled in overlapping fan folds, dedicated to some current singer of the week, with numberless copies of the matching album cover, folded and stapled and twisted across the floor and up the sides of the display area. The effect was often really rather dramatic. Raven Records was a pleasure to walk into always, interesting sounds on the P.A., rarely too many people to make a crowd but always one or two to provoke a mild and friendly debate as to the merits of this or that band, this or that style, this or that music era.

Gary, who seemed to staff the shop almost single-handed, was wiry and thin and tall with flame red hair in huge waves of curls that flowed all round him like an angel. He really should have been painted by Burne-Jones. To me Gary vividly suggested the Irish rock guitarist Rory Gallagher in his glorious prime, but without the sweat-streaks running down his cheeks. Gary was a recovering junkie who had now crash landed successfully back on planet Earth at least in part because of his time with the *Response* magazine. It was there we had first met a year or so previously. I would pass through Raven Records at least every fortnight or so, and on one occasion I told him how much I disliked having to trudge back to Oxford – well, Charlgrove – at the end of a day in London.

'There's a couch in the living room where I stay,' he volunteered immediately. 'You could doss down there. Wanna see it?'

This turned out to be the perfect solution. Only a street or two away Gary and his girlfriend had their own bedroom in a flat on the third floor that they were sharing with a pair of flatmates. The flat was a roomy, three-bedroom affair. The lounge was large with plenty of light, a dining table, a telly, a biggish sofa. The couch was usually a bit rumpled looking, from last night's telly and beers session or whatever, but it was perfectly serviceable. Gary showed me where he kept his spare bed linen, and suggested I come by the shop to borrow the keys any time I needed to crash for the night. Since I was often out late at the movies anyway, I rarely found the lounge occupied in the evening when I wanted to sleep, I never stayed more than two consecutive nights in any one week, and that rarely, so I was not too omnipresent as a non-paying guest. I did not expect breakfast but was welcome to help myself to whatever I wanted.

It was the perfect arrangement, and I was very careful not to abuse it. Whenever I was having a day off in London, now I had the choice of a late bus back to Oxford and a final bus to Charlgrove, or to stay the night in Gary's lounge and then take a 9.00am bus to get me to work for 10.30am in Oxford. Whenever I dropped by the shop Gary was always welcoming, sometimes offering an invitation to an evening meal with him and Laura, sometimes suggesting I hang around and listen to some new record that he thought would be to my taste.

Back at the Phoenix Cinema the bird was definitely not arising towards the sun, reborn. Rather, Barry was becoming steadily more dissipated. Looking back, it seems amazing to me that I didn't urge him to seek help or seek help for him myself. He of course was gruff and incommunicative at all times, quick to find fault, and always unpredictable as to his response to any remark, request, situation or challenge. He was exhausted, surly and drunk by turns, and increasingly often all three together. Somehow the cinema kept operating as a business, and we had no major lapses of accounting. Barry was happy enough to make modest informal adjustments to any of the business records to have his various tallies balance, but he never pilfered, so far as I could see. He always paid for his own drinks with his own money. Barry's shambling brusqueness always promised violence to any and all, but, in fact, his bad temper almost never went beyond a chronic incivility. The months rolled gloomily along, with we two avoiding each other, and I doing what little I could to sustain or repair staff and public relations.

One day when I was delivering the weekly returns to the Coopers at head office I was summoned to Kitty's office. As I came in, she said, without preamble,

'What's this item for taxis on the Oxford accounts? Someone is putting through for a £3.50 cab ride at least once every week. Some weeks it happens twice! What on earth is going on?'

I was completely unprepared for this, but I was also incensed. Perhaps it was that I could endure such aggression from one boss but not from two.

'Those are the taxis that take me the twelve miles home to my bed after the late shows,' I said. 'Other nights it's the last long slow local bus. Barry drives his own car. I have no car and I could not find an affordable place to stay any closer to Oxford.'

I looked at her steadily.

'I see,' she paused. 'But this really can't go on you know – what about a bicycle?'

'What about it? Twelve miles at night through unlit country lanes? Is that a serious suggestion, Kitty?'

I was amazed at how angry I was and knew that in a minute I would start shouting. She looked at me steadily but didn't look at all perturbed.

'Well, we'll have to find another solution soon.' She gazed at me sourly.

At that moment I knew immediately that I wanted another job. As I left her office, I was already planning my campaign. Was she threatening me, was she really unaware of Barry, the managerial time-bomb that was ticking away in Oxford? Did I care to tell her – or Charles? I went back to Oxford late that afternoon, fuming quietly.

The Screen on the Green before restoration 1980

83 Upper Street has a long history of film exhibition. The Pesaresi brothers used a vacant shop there from 1910. The current building, designed by Boreham & Gidding, was opened in 1913, a purpose-built cinema following the regulations set by the Cinematograph Act 1909. Named the Empress from 1913 to 1951 and the Rex from 1951 to 1970, it was used by both the local Turkish and Greek populations. Mainline Pictures Group purchased it in 1970 and carried out a complete refurbishment in 1981. It was sold to the Everyman Media Group in 2008.

Cinema Theatre Association Archive

The Screen on the Green, Islington Summer 1980

Then something unexpected happened. An advertisement appeared in *Time Out* magazine for a cinema manager. It was for one of the Coopers' direct competitors, the Screen on the Green cinema in Islington.

'Experience essential' the small-boxed advert concluded. I wasn't sure what other attributes I might have but experience of running an art-house independent I certainly had. I was pretty sure I could get both Jeff at the Pullman and James Quinn to give me a reference each if I were to ask them for one. I rang the number, got the further details, sent in a CV and within a week I had a phone call asking me to attend for an interview at Mainline Pictures offices in Museum Street.

Romaine Hart was a businesswoman with an interesting history. Legend had it that she had inherited the Rex Cinema just opposite Islington Green as her share of a grandparent's property portfolio. Romaine was a small pugnacious figure of an entrepreneur who, from one hall, was to build up a small circuit of about seven cinemas, three of them in London, that would become well renowned for good programming and up-to-date appearance and presentation.

She began with the Rex, a shabby flea-pit of a single hall of 400 or so very dirty seats on the edge of the then much less fashionable Islington area of London. Romaine had taken it on, refitted it completely and renamed it The Screen on the Green. She developed it into one of the really imaginative art-houses of London, which showed quite a cutting-edge programme of new filmmakers and risky specialist titles. She had good taste and the films she booked sold well in the main. She was quite happy to try precarious titles or subjects or themes. Sometimes she misjudged the public's appetite for experiment or controversy, but more often the films she showed earned good reviews in the right places and the public flowed in.

She'd had a huge hit with *Annie Hall*. Famously, the distributor United Artists had asked the journalists who had written glowing reviews for the film at the Edinburgh Film Festival earlier that year to promise to re-review the film when it opened in London several months later, before going nationwide. When the papers kept their word Woody Allen's film was a huge hit and Romaine's gamble paid off. In fact, the film was so popular that the film was taken on by the mainstream chains as well. *Annie Hall* may be hard to perceive as any kind of a risk today, but in 1979 Woody Allen had a faithful following only on the Upper West Side of Manhattan and in a very few university towns in the USA – all of them a long way from Islington.

More risky still was a double bill of *Tell Them Willie Boy is Here* and *Two Lane Blacktop*. One of them is a now-forgotten piece of liberalism starring Robert Redford written by a former Hollywood black-listee, the other a resolutely anti-dramatic tale of outlaw sports-car racing that collapses into un-American nihilism at its end. Both these were typical of films that Romaine Hart positioned to become very decent art-house hits in London in the 1970s and 1980s.

Since I had seen a good many of the films she had brought to London in the previous three years, and since I was at least modestly competent at the basics of the job as well as comparatively young and very keen, it is perhaps small wonder that we closed the deal there and then. I was offered about £75 a week and 1½% of sales and felt very satisfied. Mortgage tenants were always being sought in London in those days, so I was not unduly anxious about finding somewhere to live.

The Screen on Islington Green, to give it its full title, was always attractively scruffy, unlike the rather vitiated and hung-over look of the Pullman in Chelsea or the Phoenix in Oxford and attracted a very reliable crowd of the Islington chattering classes. Titles like *Picnic at Hanging Rock* and *Babette's Feast* always did very well there. These were standard Oscar bait of the foreign film variety, and so dependent on a good broadsheet review, but easy to promote otherwise.

A particular speciality of the Green's programming was youth trash. In the popular culture of the 70s there was a precise point at which rock and roll and genre cinema intersected. When that happens successfully, even today, a lot of money is to be made from films which were often low cost to make. Examples from the 70s would be Kathryn Bigelow's *The Loveless* or the original *Repo Man* with Emilio Estevez, also Sam Rami's *The Evil Dead* and its even noisier sequel *Evil Dead II*, as well as Tobe Hooper's banned *Texas Chainsaw Massacre* and David Lynch's still uniquely unclassifiable *Eraserhead*. All these were hits at the Green, drawing crowds for weeks, and then returning on late-night double bills for nigh on decades afterwards. Understand: a cinema cannot create a hit, but if the paying public feels a natural fit between the film, the hall and its local constituency, then a reputation for reliable and regular diversion can be built up which is of great benefit to the hall itself.

This ecological balance between an independent hall, its particular regional sub-sets of regular viewers and the specific films screened, has been decreasingly present for quite some time. There are very few local cinemas these days that (Covid permitting) I might attend regularly where I might confidently expect an accurate awareness of a local audience and see it reflected in the films programmed for that site.

There might be numerous reasons for this, but undoubtedly the magnificent diffusion of film culture in the last thirty years has been consequent upon the development of first VHS and then DVD recordings. Nowadays home streaming means that it is now possible to see, to study, to evaluate and effectively to re-read an enormous range of films from near and far, from now and past, from good to bad – so what need to traipse out to sit in an expensive dingy hall and listen to other people cough and whisper and chew and check their phones for emails and texts while you strain to read subtitles? Plenty of people would rather drink a glass of wine or two at home and slump in front of a good-sized telly. I like to go to the cinema, and still do so regularly. But nowadays, I'm a member of a shrinking minority.

That day I left Romaine's office with the job in my hand. I told her that I would have to give a month's notice but that if I could get away sooner, I would let her know immediately. I rang Kitty's number but Charles picked up. He was very bewildered asking me if I was sure I was being wise and had I thought through the consequences of my decision and so on. I was firm and blithe. The following week there were two phone messages from Kitty's office but I determined to ignore them. If she really wanted me, she would keep trying and we would speak. Till then I'd wait. When I told Barry I was moving on to a manager slot in London he looked no more disgusted than usual. 'Not surprised' was about the full extent of his commentary. The ladies downstairs were really rather sweet: 'Oh Mr Scudamore, we's only jes' got used to you,' said Mrs Harris. This seemed to be the consensus and was at least expressed tenderly by most of those present.

I was very busy in my few remaining days off – the ones that weren't truncated by Barry's need to have a few extra hours away 'to wait in for the TV repair man' and the like. When I looked round my room at Charlgrove I realised that in steadily bringing things each weekend from London – extra frying pans and dictionaries and Rolling Stones LPs and the like – I seemed to have accumulated a great deal of impedimenta which I must now return to the metropolis. I would have to take 90% of what I couldn't part with back to Mum's and hope for the best. I had also to find somewhere to live. I knew that I would be fine for a few nights on Gary's couch, but that would be a fortnight at the very outside.

I made several trips to Oxfam over the next few days. My Charlgrove housemates accepted most of the kitchen kit I was ready to part with. The books and records and more wearable clothes I stored in my old bedroom back at my mum's; my old room had evolved by now into a nondescript dumping space used by the entire family, so no one was incommoded. I camped at Gary's and lived out of a hold-all. In the Islington local free sheet – delivered to the Screen on the Green – I saw an advert for a room to rent in a flat only two streets away. I had the presence of mind to write my application and details to the flat owner on Screen on the Green headed notepaper and to push it through the letterbox on my journey home from work during my first week. That did the trick. I now had a room to live in, no travel costs whatever, and a new job that was a real step up. How lucky can a man be?

The Green was in one sense simply a generic art-house/second release single hall. But the sense of local commitment, the depth and range of the regulars, was exceptional. There were old-school film buffs, all dandruff and thermos flasks; there were be-spiked Goths along with various sub-sets of intellectual punks; there were art school dandies in their gloriously retro-fitted oversize overcoats and hand-painted pixie-boots; there were slightly battered skinhead and suedehead couples, both in matching braces and boots, him with fewer teeth than her; there were assistant editors of *Granta* in well-rubbed biker jackets. Whenever a specific film provoked it there would be an outbreak of couples in well-cut linen and wool with expensive shoes whom I suspected of being commissioning editors for television. Many of those faces I was to see over and over again in the following months.

The staff was equally varied. As ever there was the steady trickle of replaced and replaceable youngsters who tore tickets and sold ice-creams for a few weeks. But there was also an established cadre of longer serving workers. At the head was Colin Payne, the chief projectionist. He was a large, well-framed man with thick black hair and brows, a look of mild disbelief upon his face at all times. He had thick wrists, dark hair on the back of his hands, and fingers that were blunt and rounded but very agile and delicate. He was courteous, hard-working, efficient, and orderly. His characteristic stance was to lean back slightly with a large hand on either hip and look at you very attentively.

Colin's projection suite was a delight to visit; it was tidy and well swept, with all the shelves labelled and the film cans neatly stacked. The suite was dominated by the two huge projectors that rattled very loudly as the film strips passed through their gates. (The gate holds the film strip in front of the projector's lens.) There was the smell of hot metal and warm oil. Conversing was a matter of shouting over the din of the machines, exactly like being in a ship's engine room. But I always admired the neat rows of much-used tools, each in its bracket upon the wall above the workbench and was stirred by the truck and tackle and gear of Colin's work. Though often pressed, Colin was rarely flustered.

Prints could sometimes be delivered late or damaged or incomplete. He could be assembling the reels of some new European release and find that the tally of parts was incorrect – with the film due to go on in ninety minutes; or the projector bulb would blow in the minutes before an important press show; or the take-up spool would lose its slack and the print would run tight in the gate and start to judder with every probability that it would burn. Colin almost always found a way to jury-rig a repair or acquire a replacement part or print whatever the crisis, even on a Sunday afternoon or during Christmas week when all the technical suppliers would be closed for ten days.

Eventually even Colin grew to be aware of how much Romaine was relying on him to fetch and carry, to maintain and replace – far beyond the bounds of what might be routinely expected of a chief projectionist. She was, however, also given to occasional bouts of brusque behaviour, no doubt whenever she felt sorely tried in some other quarter. From this perhaps derived the local legend that was widely reported to me of Colin's grand plan to resign from the Screen on the Green's projection suite.

Colin had at last come to feel that he had been presumed upon once too often, and was too little appreciated by Romaine, so he determined to seek alternative employment with better hours and more defined responsibilities. He had seen that London Transport was seeking both bus drivers and mechanics and applied for an interview, attended and passed a technical test as well as a driving test, and was offered a position to start in a month. Colin held to his new resolution, and the next time Romaine visited the cinema he advised her that he would be leaving, after seventeen years' service, on the 12th of the next month. Reportedly she was dumbfounded and said she didn't believe him. Colin showed her his letter of acceptance – she held the page in her hand and still protested that it was not possible. The story went on that she rang him daily asking him to reconsider, that she asked him to interview and appoint his replacement which he refused to do. She offered him a rise, then a further rise, then guaranteed set hours and extra paid holiday. Colin was determined that he'd had enough and that he would leave. The climax came with less than a week of Colin's term of notice remaining. Romaine, legend insisted, had gone up to the projection box and literally got down on her knees and begged Colin not to leave – the whole place would collapse without him, the business would be ruined, she and her two daughters would starve. It was a legendary appeal, by all accounts. And Romaine won. Colin stayed. He ran the projection box and all matters relating to it with as much care as ever, and Romaine almost never took him for granted again. She was never shy about giving out commands, but to Colin, her orders always ended with a glance up to his face and a 'please'.

Romaine had an administrative assistant-cum-second-in-command called Roger Austin. He was rangy and limber and quick-tempered. He was the first young man I knew to wear his head shaved. At this time Romaine had been expanding her business to include at least two more cinemas in central London – one of which was a new single hall on Haverstock Hill called, logically enough, the Screen on the Hill. She had enlarged her business in another, very important, way also. She had set up a distribution arm for her company called Mainline Pictures. That is, she intended to bid directly for the territorial rights to any suitable film at any trade show or festival she went to. If the terms were right she would have complete control of the title for a set period of time and thus would earn back all of the potential profit on its release. Mainline would have to plan and bear much of the cost of the promotion and advertising, but her cinemas would have a supply of carefully chosen titles that she could release as and when she deemed the moment most auspicious.

Romaine and Roger had to work this balancing act between them which required close cooperation and careful planning. Roger also ran the late-night bookings for the 'Screen' circuit. This was effectively the same job as I had been doing back in my days at the Paris Pullman. Roger booked a single title for Thursday nights and then a double bill for every Friday and Saturday late show. The films were booked at a flat fee for around £100 a title, so even with the house's basic overheads to find it was not impossible to show a modest profit on such programming.

Only the difference here was that Roger wanted always to book double bills and the combined length of these never seemed to matter: *Apocalypse Now* teamed with *The Deerhunter* was a popular programme of his. Pairing *The Godfather* and *The*

Godfather Part II was another. Starting soon after 11.30pm and allowing for a ten minute interval this is a 3.45am finish in anybody's money. After these and similar programmes had happened a few times, I protested to Roger that this was absurdly late, and that indeed something between a quarter and a fifth of the audience would leave at the interval and almost a full third of the remainder during the final half hour of the latter feature. Roger was entirely unconvinced: 'S'not long, s'not long at all,' he would sneer. Of course, it makes no difference financially when people leave a show – they've paid the full price up front. And I would always release any staff after the interval, which would be at about 1.30am. Colin and I were paid an overtime rate for the later hours, but I could still fall into my bed exhausted at 4.15am two nights a week. Since I was on duty from 10.30am each workday morning this could make for an extraordinarily long day, twice times sixteen hours if both the Friday and the Saturday late shows fell to me on my rota. I used to drop off to sleep vengefully thinking that I should telephone Roger at home right now, at dawn's first light, to tell him that I just got home and see if it was not so late to him then. But I never had the nerve.

A few of the late shows were in themselves memorable. Whenever we showed any of the punk 'rockumentaries' or David Bowie movies or Elvis Presley double bills that particular youth sub-set would attend in strength. I would have Colin play appropriate background music through the P.A. as the house filled; there would be a lot of cheery half-drunk chatter and a fog of (mostly) cigarette smoke. At 11.30pm the lights would dim and there would a growling shout of gleeful anticipation as the curtains parted. When all went well the crowd would mostly subside as the evening wore on into the night, soothed by the effects of prior alcohol and subsequent sugary drinks and chocolate. With a comedy double bill, two Woody Allens or two Marilyn Monroes perhaps, it was rather pleasant to sit in my little office which was set into the void behind the screen (exactly as the Pullman had been configured, in that respect) and hear the waves of laughing and barks and shrieks of surprised delight over the rumbling boom of the nearside speakers as the film rattled along.

Far more wearing were the horror double bills such as *Night of the Living Dead* with *The Texas Chainsaw Massacre*. In *Massacre* Marilyn Burns plays a teenage girl character who screams in despair for her very life as she is pursued through all of the last forty minutes of Tobe Hooper's dire masterpiece; she screams forte-fortissimo over an essentially assaultive cacophony of grinding and roaring industrial noise and electronic-music-as-noise effects. Hers are the shattering cries of final utter terror, ululating a-rhythmically and hugely magnified, screams that you cannot escape from, that go on and on, like some sonic punishment invented by a CIA-trained torturer. Screams and screams, expressive of the primal fear that can end only with the silence of annihilation. In my little hutch behind the screen, under such bedlam, trying to tot up a row of figures for next Friday's pay packets was testing work.

On one late-night show the print itself was incomplete and I feared the ravening mob that would spend itself at last upon my own primal screams. Roger Austin had booked for that Saturday night a double bill of *Major Dundee* and *The Wild Bunch*, two rowdy Sam Peckinpah westerns. The problem was that nearly 300 feet of the final reel of the latter film was not in the can when Colin came to make up the film for projection. *The Wild Bunch* has, as its justly legendary climax, an extended and slaughterous shoot-out. The effect is at once loud, balletic, sanguinary and apocalyptic. And it was now Saturday afternoon and the distributor and the film store at Denham were both locked shut for the weekend. One solution would be simply to show *Major Dundee* and not bother with the incomplete second title. But *The Wild Bunch* was definitely the top card, the star billing of that particular programme. Not to show it seemed pusillanimous, somehow. I told Colin to make up both films ready for projection and that I would make an address to the audience before the screening. In the relative calm of Saturday afternoon this seemed a plan both plausible and reasonable. All that week we had had a grim Ingmar Bergman, *The Serpent's*

Egg, for our main programme, so a very subdued audience had crept out at the end of every showing for the past seven days.

But as 11.30pm approached that Saturday night, I began to feel more and more doubtful about my plan. The usual half-drunk, half-hysterical mob began to file into the hall. Rather gloomily I could see that Roger had again anticipated his public well and that we were to be largely full this night. At 11.35pm I walked down the aisle from the back of the hall and then across into the centre space between the front row of seats and the screen.

With the curtains behind me I surveyed the crowd. 'Don't let them smell your fear,' I thought as I looked at this roiling mass of dishevelled humanity. As Colin faded down the non-sync music I looked at my customers steadily. They had now perceived that something unconventional was afoot.

'Good evening,' I began with as much professional and civil gusto as I could bring to bear, 'I have some bad news.'

In reply there was a universal and theatrical groan. Then bellows: 'Bollocks!' 'Get on with it!' 'Start the fucking film' was the immediate consensual response. I was reminded of the jungle at moonrise, the beasts glaring and tussling at the water-hole.

I shouted back at them,

'We do not have the end of *The Wild Bunch*. The film is incomplete and we cannot get hold of the rest of it. We are missing the final ten minutes. If you do not want to see an incomplete film take your ticket stub to the box office now and they will refund your money immediately. Once the programme starts there will be no refunds. Miss the end of *The Wild Bunch* or get a refund now. Those are your options.'

Followed now much slurred debate amongst the citizenry. Some were for going, some were for staying. Groups had internal debates about whether they should all go or all stay. None were happy. Perhaps the least befuddled decided to leave and to get their money back as promised. Even these, however, were too relaxed to work out that they needed to present the correct change with their stubs, in order to achieve a whole banknote in exchange. The tired cashier did her best, but we soon ran out of change, the queue did not diminish for quite a while and an atmosphere of ill-temper thickened throughout the process. I signalled Colin to start the film well before the refunds were complete because the atmosphere in the hall now was of the calm before a riot. The programme began, the dark seeming to soothe one and all.

The refunds were finally completed. Wendy, the cashier, was pink-eyed, nearly tearful. I felt very drained, yet the evening had really only just begun. As *Major Dundee* spooled through the projector gate a sense of routine re-established itself: the audience settled, the horses galloped, the guns fired, the first film ended. The interval was the familiar queues for paper cups of coffee and chocolate or nut bars. *The Wild Bunch* began. It's an eventful film, full of riding and dust and betrayals, of drunken self-pitying reminiscence and violent arguments with mortal consequences. I was in dread of the sudden truncated end, the way the final bloody deaths of the four anti-heroes would be abbreviated, absent in effect, and the result this might produce upon the largish remnant of the crowd that had remained until the film's abrupt end. In the event there was nothing. On the screen the cacophonous pell-mell of mass slaughter and multiple death ceased abruptly in mid-din. The ragged end of the film strip slipped through the projector gate. A white flare filled the hall. Colin shut off the machine and faded the house lights up quickly. Silence. There was a huge collective jerk and groan of disappointment, and then every somnambulist soul gathered its wraps and shuffled silently away.

Sometimes it wasn't the film that provoked an unexpected challenge. On one occasion it was the very nature of the audience itself. For some years the wonderful musical / gangster tale of *The Harder They Come* had been a late-night staple on the programme at the Green. This film is a legend: in 1972 it was the first break-out hit of Jamaican cinema, it stars Jimmy Cliff as a country boy who comes to the capital Kingston to make it big as a singer but who is taken advantage of by everyone he meets. He evolves into a gangster and dies shooting at the corrupt police as they surround him. It's a classic 'good bad man' fable, the music is wonderful and the ending exciting, inevitable and tragic. In 1972 for many non-Jamaicans this film was an early exposure to Jamaican music and popular culture. A few years further on Bob Marley would consolidate this in his own way, but that would be later.

Film distributors are always on the look-out for the next big thing, and if it can be a cheap-at-the-outset, get-in-on-the-ground-floor, next big thing, then so much the better. Romaine acquired the rights to a Jamaican film called *Rockers*. This was another tale of cheeky bad behaviour set in the Jamaican underworld, but this time with a variety of actual musical acts and stars appearing in it, each performing a musical number in their own particular style. Horsemouth Wallace and Gregory Isaacs were two acts that appeared. *Rockers* had the most wonderful strap line on its poster. Under the title ran the superb poetic warning: 'I's like a steppin' razor, don't you watch I size, I dangerous.'

Rockers was advertised in the London West Indian press and elsewhere and news spread fast. Soon we had queues of folk, many come up from Ladbroke Grove and Westbourne Park and Brixton, in an untidy line, stretching around the block. Everyone was cheery and good-humoured, so long as it didn't rain. But the notion of waiting for the start of the next programme in order to enter seemed an alien concept. It didn't really matter for the early and mid-week houses, but every afternoon and all evenings of the week we would have a line of mainly young West Indian Londoners and their pals very unimpressed about having to stand about in the street to wait their turn to go in. I would come down the line to count and to reassure and then to advise late joiners of the queue that they were unlikely to be admitted that night. The tall dignified Rastas, in their green and yellow and red knitted hats, would shake their heads dolefully: 'Ah maan, I an' I can' stan' up awl dis lang time, maan,' they would reproach me. Everyone wanted to get in, everyone would protest that their mates were already within and so therefore they too must, perforce, be admitted. No matter how earnestly I assured them that I had a capacity house, that there simply were no more seats to sell, the general consensus was that it was all a trick to cheat them out of their fun. They were gloomy and they grumbled, and they were loath to leave.

This situation was compounded in that some people didn't want to leave when the film was over – 'Nah, maan, I come late time y'know, I din' see awl de ting, now. Me rest heah.' Of course, if anyone did come out of the show during a performance there would be a surge towards the front, as though the exit of two meant there must now be space for twenty more. And then there was a further refinement: someone coming out might recognise a friend – a group of friends – and immediately decide to re-join them, but not at the back of the queue, but rather to re-join the queue alongside their friends. This would often lead to angry expostulations by those around about. These were situations I was not about to police if I could avoid it, though in fairness I don't believe anyone ever asked me to.

Inside the hall things were rarely calmer. All 400 seats had been sold, but this was not the crowd that sat silently through Ingmar Bergman's harrowing tales of spiritual desperation and psychological collapse, sniffing faintly through the final minutes.

No, here were shouts of glee and roars of approval at all examples of telling authority what to do with itself, cheers for gunplay, loud shouts of approval whenever some righteous music started or played. Everyone was having a very noisy, very convivial time. The air was thick with the smell of ganja but no one was complaining. There were also a lot of cans of Red Stripe beer in evidence, notwithstanding that we had no licence to sell any beer whatsoever. I felt that, here, discretion was the better part of valour. Business was chaotic but very good, and though it was an exhausting four-week run, it was quite exhilarating in its way.

But now my cleaners nearly revolted in a body. About ten days into *Rockers*' run, all three of them came to me. This was unusual because the cleaners began work very early every morning and finished before 10.00am and so I rarely saw them. But today they had a complaint, so they waited for the manager. The hall was very messy, they insisted, much worse than usual. 'Is too mush working,' Renata, the spokesperson, insisted. They had cleaned the hall so they had nothing to show me. I reminded them that we were doing three capacity houses every day and four such on weekends just at the moment but that the current level of business would inevitably run down in two more weeks or so. The cleaners were not very impressed and said that they would not work if the present level of mess continued.

'What is the matter, exactly?' I asked.

'Too mush mess, too mush…' Renata repeated, with the others nodding sadly.

I suggested I come in to see for myself at 8.30am the following morning. This would be a bit of an effort for me, but their complaint was well out of the run of ordinary grumbles.

The following morning, I crept in at 8.32am. Renata seemed quite surprised, then relieved, that I had appeared. Perhaps she had not believed me when I had said that I would come in early. Long experience with managers promising more than they meant, or than they even intended, perhaps. She led me to the right side of the hall about halfway down. I could easily see for myself there was indeed a richer tilth of litter on the carpeting than was common. But up on this end was something genuinely unusual: a wide loam of some powdery yellow-brown organic substance, quite three inches deep, lay upon the floor. It spread for about four rows and into the aisles in front and behind. This strange yellow mess was glazed more thinly and widely all over the entire cinema floor but was concentrated just here in a thicker layer. It appeared to be of a dry consistency and had only a faintly musty odour. Very gingerly, I knelt down to look more closely. I could now see this was a sea of small fragments of some organic shape, dimpled, curved, irregular. I put out my hand, too late thinking of a glove, and picked some of it up. It was dry, yellowy, fibrous.

Suddenly I understood. These were fragments of monkey-nuts shells – peanut shells. These crushed shells were all across the hall, stamped into the carpets, and had been carried by customers' shoes to virtually all the floor surfaces of the building. What had happened here? True, we sold peanuts at our concession stand, but any peanuts we sold were in clean packets, the nuts salted and already shelled. And by the look of what I could see there would have been enough shells for about two years' supply of our nuts…

'How long has this been going on?' I asked Renata.

She looked at the other ladies who were looking at the mess at the hall and at me with increasing concern. Clearly they feared being held to blame for this bizarre occurrence.

'Four days, maybe five days,' she said very earnestly. The others nodded when she looked at them.

'I don't understand,' I said, 'but clean it all up please, and I will watch carefully. Something strange is happening. I will watch.'

I kept my language simple and my tone neutral. Something very odd indeed must be happening. It was more than possible for cleaners to grow a bit slack in their duties, but no cleaners could ignore this amount of filth and then draw the manager's attention to it. It defied logic and it was inconvenient.

At 1.00pm that day we opened for the first house as usual. There was a short but cheery and excited queue waiting even as the shutter in front of the door was raised to let them in. Everyone filed in, paid up and settled down. We were not full at all though the numbers were well up for a mid-week afternoon. I watched quietly. There didn't seem to be anything happening that was unusual. As the house ended, I walked all around. There were the usual 'stay-overs' in the audience but not many and no trouble. Some litter certainly, but nothing untoward. The day wore on, the house now filling right up and this necessitating much management of the crowds and the staff and re-supplies of stock to the sales counter and change to the box office. About 8.00pm, just a bit before the final house, I set off, on patrol, around the hall.

There it was! A modest silt of mashed monkey-nut shells, not anywhere near as deep as this morning, but very evident nonetheless, lay covering the carpeting along several rows in the middle of the hall, spreading out into the centre of the right aisle. I was dumbfounded. Who could have eaten and spread so many nuts, and where had they come from anyway? I resolved to spend the whole of the final house in the hall to see if I could watch this mystery unfold before me. I warned Wendy at the cash desk and Colin in the box that I would be in the hall and was not to be disturbed for anything less than a flash flood or the Second Coming.

I stood at the back quietly. The house was full, the film lively, and the audience happy, so there was naturally quite a bit of coming and going, to the toilets, to the sweetie counter, whatever. About fifteen minutes into the film everyone was smoking, rolling up, re-lighting, passing lights to friends. Some were even smoking cigarettes. Then I noticed, through the haze of activity, a small flickering but persistent light. Was someone selling joints, perhaps? Too risky surely – anyway this crowd came well supplied with all the extra entertainments they wanted: Red Stripe beers, Jamaican patties, cold jerk chicken, I shouldn't wonder.

I wanted to find out about this continual flickering light that seemed to bother no one. I walked quietly down the side of the hall. There was a tall Rasta in a floor length trench coat standing with his back to me in the aisle. He seemed to be at the centre of whatever was transpiring. Next to him was a pal who was whispering loudly to the crowd and taking change from hands as it was passed to him. He was passing something back. I came a little closer. There was so much noise from the soundtrack and the general hubbub of the crowd that my game of grandmother's footsteps was really rather surplus to requirements. But then I saw. The taller Rasta was standing over a half-hundredweight gunny sack which he was holding open in front of him. He had sold nearly all of his monkey nuts already, as I could clearly see by the light of the bicycle lamp that he and his pal were using to simplify their negotiations with their clientele.

At the end of the film, I stood at the back of the hall and watched the two entrepreneurs come slowly up the aisle towards the back. They were both very tall, it seemed to me.

'Evening, gentlemen, I'm the manager,' said I, looking up at them and beginning to feel rather uncertain. 'Business was good, I think?'

They both glanced at my face, then exchanged a look. The one holding the crumpled empty sack smiled quietly down at me.

'Nuttin' t' git vex' about, maan,' he said, politely dismissive.

I tried to appear managerial:

'Gentlemen, look at the mess behind you, it's a lot to clean up isn't it?'

To my surprise they did both stop and turn to regard the uneven trample of nut shells that spread deeply all about where they had been prospering just minutes earlier.

'True, maan, true – we nah come agin.'

They smiled graciously and swept past me with a swish of their long coats. Later, after the hall was empty, I got a black plastic bag and a dustpan and brush and swept the majority of the mess away. I left a note assuring the cleaners that the nut shells would not re-occur. They didn't.

These were busy days and nights, and Romaine was delighted with the returns. I said that the staff were working hard. She gave us all a cheery wave, but nothing more. Wendy, the cashier, was very pressed during those busy weeks, but she didn't falter. She was a slim, neat brunette, with a dancer's figure and grey eyes, said to be studying both music and psychology. I couldn't think how. She was at the cinema a lot of the time and usually looked tired when she left. I decided I would like to know her better but she was always quite unimpressed by any conversational gambits I made. Courteous, always, even friendly, in a cool way but always unmoved by me. (I remember I even went back six months after I was no longer working at the Green to see if she would now rise to my bait. But she swam quite away, a cool dark flicker at the bottom of her own clear pond.)

Then there was the robbery. One evening later that summer I was in the kiosk and box-office area (they were neighbouring undivided spaces) just readying the takings for reconciliation, and then deposit in the local bank's night safe, when the door to the sales area was suddenly shouldered open. A young man, pale as a corpse, in a denim jacket glowered at me. He was holding a table knife that had been crudely sharpened to a point. His sleeve cuffs were worn and faded, his face hollow with panicky desperation. I was alone and very shocked. It had been a quiet evening and I had sent the cashier off home only minutes previously. 'Shut up, jus' fuckin' shut up,' he whispered hoarsely. There was no one around and I had not said a word. He quickly advanced into the paybox, grabbed up the two bundles of banknotes off the counter, shoved them into his jacket. He jerked the knife blade toward my face. I stood silent and rigid. He backed very rapidly away, keeping his eyes fixed on me. At the doorway he turned and bolted. I stood there alone and blinking. The act had been so utterly sudden and I had been quite unprepared for it.

In another thirty seconds Colin passed by the paybox on some routine mission of his own, and I croaked out to him,

'We've been robbed.'

He was quicker than I.

'Which way did they go? How many?' he asked in an urgent hiss.

I reassured him that there was but one lad and that he now had at least a minute's start on any pursuer. Colin skipped out onto the pavement and had a long look in both directions up and down the late evening of Islington's Upper Street. I believe he would have set off to run after anyone that looked likely. But there was no one. As my fright wore off I felt increasingly sick at heart and very ashamed of myself. I felt I had let myself down badly; it would have been more professional to have insisted that the cashier stay on with me for that final three or four minutes as I readied the takings and locked away the sales area. Why hadn't I at least yelled out – or just run after him myself? I wished I could have presented the really rather pathetic figure of the robber as a more formidable opponent. Of course I rang the police from the box-office telephone and reported the incident, and then immediately afterwards dialled Romaine's home number. To be fair to her she did first ask if I was unhurt, but there was a sullen silence when she asked me how much had been taken and I had to say that I would have to balance off the day returns to give a precise figure but at the moment I thought about £700. I hung up.

Within another three minutes a police car turned up and two muscular young cops bounced briskly into the foyer.

'Which way'd 'e go? Got any description, Sir?' they asked enthusiastically.

Since I could offer very little they were soon gone, in the direction of the nearest housing estate. In another ten minutes the house emptied at the end of the film, and in fifteen minutes more I went off towards my home and my bed feeling more than usually spent. The following day there were further questions from a police team as well as an investigator for the insurance company. Both were civil enough. For both I recited the salient details and re-enacted them as a sort of one-person mime show. They seemed satisfied when they went away. Within a week a brand-new floor drop-safe had been fitted in the kiosk and the old street-level wall safe, that had been clearly visible from the public pavement, had been effectively rendered obsolete. But from that moment on I believe Romaine never really trusted me again. I don't mean that she suspected me of being complicit in the crime, but she suspected me of being careless – and in that I couldn't challenge her then nor can I now.

But being a manager wasn't always threats or mysterious accidents. One day that summer I received a phone call from Roger Austin the programmer (he of the epic late-night programmes) sounding unusually excited. 'You are going to have a secret test screening next week. The print will be delivered the night before. The show will be the 6 o'clock house next Wednesday.' So we were to offer a 'test screening' to an audience. I wondered what the film could be. Test screenings are common practice at cinemas in the Los Angeles valley area. The idea is that a very recently completed film is simply plopped in front of a cinema audience and then the studio gets to see how well the film plays in front of a paying crowd: do they laugh in the right places, are the sad scenes weepy enough, do the stunts make the crowd gasp, do the explosions look impressive, are folk satisfied at the end? Often a film will be subsequently re-edited to minimise a perceived shortcoming, a secondary character's part may cut way down or the heroine given extra close-ups to boost her performance; more occasionally whole new endings are written and shot.

The audience are told as they go into the hall that the film that they have paid to see will not be screened but that instead 'a major studio' will be showing 'a major new release' and that they will be asked to fill in a card at the end. They are at liberty not to attend and to have a refund if they cannot wait for the next house, of course. Usually people do stay, driven by natural curiosity perhaps, and of course if the film is in any way worthy, you have the very contemporary boast of telling your friends wherever you go for the next three months 'Oh that new George Clooney movie due out the month after next – I've seen it already. It's pretty cool' thus basking in all the dimly reflected glory you can, so excitingly, muster.

In truth, by the time the following Wednesday rolled around, I was pretty excited myself. This would be a decided departure from ordinary routine and who knew what the film would be? But I hoped it would be something remarkable and British and entirely new. As I remember we had a very decent crowd that evening, filing in for Woody Allen's *Annie Hall* now in about the fifth week of its very successful run. Romaine herself was there, smiling, tense, agitated. She walked to the front and told the crowd that was just settling down for the adverts that we would not be screening the promised film (loud but theatrical groans of disappointment) but that we would instead be showing a sneak preview of a major release (mildly ironic cheers) and that they would have the huge privilege – said she determinedly – of seeing this new masterpiece before anyone else. So ticket refunds now or stay put.

The lights went down and the words *Monty Python* appeared on the screen. Immediately there was a huge shout of joy. The film was *Monty Python's Life of Brian* and the audience loved it from the opening minutes. They roared with laughter, they wept, they cheered, they sang along with the ridiculous songs: near the end, hung upon a cross between two thieves, Brian sings to the crowd below the magnificent ditty 'Always look on the bright side of life'. The crowd rocked with joy, singing along lustily. They danced onto the pavement outside after a very long film, the cut running over two and a half hours at that time. They scarcely noticed John Cleese and Michael Palin standing quietly at the very back of the hall. They, too, had both begun beaming after about the first ten minutes of the screening. They had had the relief of seeing that a very expensive and fractious gamble of a film-shoot was very likely to pay off. That was a memorable day indeed. In due time the film itself, now slightly trimmed down, mostly for crisper cuts between scenes, came to the Screen on the Green, where it enjoyed the same large success that it was to have across the nation later that year.

None the less, after the robbery Romaine wanted rid of me and began to suggest that it was time that I 'worked for a bigger company, to get more experience'. One day she told me that she wanted me to go and see a contact of hers who worked for one of the national cinema chains, Classic Cinemas. Within less than a month, I had joined Classic Cinemas and a whole new chapter was to begin.

The Classic Cinema, Tooting Bec

Designed by Norfolk & Pryor, this cinema opened in 1910 as the Central Hall Picture Palace and was refurbished and given a stunning neon exterior display and renamed the Classic in 1936. Used to screen Bollywood films on Sundays in its last years, it closed in 1983 and eventually was converted for retail use with the circle becoming a nightclub.

This image was reproduced by kind permission of London Borough of Lambeth, Archives Department SP25/951/CLA.1

The Classic Cinema, Tooting Bec Spring 1981

Mr Brown was the regional manager for Classic Cinemas, outer London area. He was commanding, overweight, and brusque. He smoked constantly and spoke in an ill-tempered growl at almost all times.

His whole demeanour said, 'Be nice to me, for I can sack you today and I just might.' This was a managerial persona that had served him perfectly well all his working life, and he was not in need of any other. The southernmost outpost of his particular region was Tooting, in south London. The elderly manager there was retiring, and Brown needed to find a replacement for him quickly. In 1981 the area of Tooting was rather run down. Later that year the area was to be convulsed by two very different events, one local, one national. The local one was the so-called Brixton riots, the national one was the marriage of Charles Windsor to Diana Spencer.

The local residents whom I remember were made up of equal parts traditional white working class (now soon to be the second generation of the chronic unemployed), Mediterranean shopkeepers, and hard-working Arabs from all over the Middle East, and a fair few South Asian families. The local businesses neighbouring the cinema, on both sides of the street, were almost all the vegetable and general grocery shops that are the economic lifeblood of immigrant families the world over. The pubs and laundrettes dotted amongst those shops were mostly shabby, with rubbed doors and grubby windows and the occasional cafes being the halal version of burger chains or else old-style original builders' fry-up joints, all steamed up windows outside and worn Formica tables within.

The Classic Tooting itself was a battered little cinema: a small hall just a few minutes' walk along Tooting Broadway that had stood on its corner site for at least seventy years. It was a single hall, with a circle above (rarely used in my day there), a 750 seater, stained brown within by years of nicotine and benign neglect, with leaky toilets and jury-rigged projectors. The staff team were three part-timers, weary belle-dames all, who appeared to have been at the Classic Tooting since VE day. They were unconvincingly aided by four narrow-eyed part-time post-adolescents who were otherwise unemployable and didn't fancy the army. The most interesting aspect of managing this slowly dying flea-pit was the crowd that came. During the week we had very unremarkable general release titles that drew an unremarkable crowd, but the weekends were dominated by two special sessions. On Friday nights at 11.00pm we would show a Kung-Fu double bill and on Sunday afternoons and evenings a pair of Bollywood musicals.

The Friday nights were controlled by Andy. Andy was Singapore Chinese by birth but had been a British citizen for many a year. He was a natural entrepreneur: seeing any business opportunity he would go for it. The chance he saw here was to make money showing specialist films that he had access to. Andy booked the Tooting Classic to show Kung-Fu movies. Kung-Fu is a genre produced (then) mainly in Hong Kong that already had a global following. They are tales of unarmed combat often set in a loosely imagined past time in China. The tales are always revenge fables because the hero may only use his paramount fighting skills to avenge a great wrong done to someone to whom he owes a debt of honour – his Kung-Fu teacher or the slain leader of his community, perhaps. The narrative is always set within strictures at least as tight of those of the western. The fights are ballets of impossible hand-to-hand fighting. Impossible in the sense that the antagonists' leaps at one another routinely defy any laws of gravity or physics. Impossible too were the actual blows exchanged between the combatants, the sound of each punch or kick being so amplified as to suggest that any single one of them would be enough to fell a mule.

The fights in these popular fables begin as group affairs – the hero has supporters – with the massed minions of the arch-enemy. Gradually as the tale progresses, the combatants on each side reduce in number, but the length of the fights extend. The climax is nearly always a very extended one-to-one set-to between the exhausted hero and the arch-enemy, a contest fought across the debris of the collapsing palace, made of break-away luxury furniture, in which the villain always lives.

Andy would present two of these tales every Friday night to a packed hall of British-born West Indian teenagers. No one else ever attended. A few pretty girlfriends, perhaps, but they were decorative rarities. The atmosphere was lively and excited always: 'the weekend starts here' kind of thing. Andy had rented the hall, so Classic Cinemas supplied a manager (me) to run the hall, instruct the projectionist, and lock up afterwards. Andy supplied the film prints and paid his own security and front-of-house staff. Being barely five feet tall Andy wasn't even as tall as I. But he was stocky and always spoke confidently. He brought three or four large lads with him every week whom I never remember speaking – except perhaps to him, and then rarely. The crowd would mill around – it was always a very disorderly queue – but good natured so long as there were no challenges. Everyone was happy until there was any suspicion that they were being slighted or taken advantage of in any way, so that ill-tempered gestures or pushes could explode into serious rows with lightning rapidity. Andy's large lads cruised unsmilingly amongst the throng in the foyer, circling like sharks, nosing for bad behaviour. This gave everyone an excuse to constrain themselves.

Still, there were incidents. Once a large angry man, shouting in the direction of someone who was just entering the hall through the double doors at the back of the foyer, tried to push past Andy. Andy chested up to the shouting man and asked him for his ticket. The man seemed unconcerned. Worse, he pushed back at Andy, loudly remonstrating. The crowd, close by, attended every move. Andy's eyes narrowed.

'You go out,' he said evenly, 'you go out now'.

The man glared down at Andy, the top of whose head was neatly under his chin.

'Ain't fuckin' goin' anywhere, mon,' the man growled down at him.

Silence in the foyer. All were now watching. Andy took one quick step back and very suddenly extended two fingers and the thumb of his right hand. Andy seemed to barely tap the man on his chest with the three fingers, his hand travelling rapidly forward and back perhaps two inches, like a viper's strike. Instantly the big fellow's face turned grey and he sank to the floor like a sack of laundry. He lay still. I was horrified and rushed over to look down at him. He was still breathing, just. Two of Andy's big lads picked him up and took him outside and sat him up against the wall. There was a collective exhalation of breath from us all, and then the evening resumed its course. Andy's tiny gesture had been alarming and impressive. I never saw it repeated.

Business was always lively on these Friday evenings, with a lot of sales at the concession stands and the double bill nearly always sold out. At the end of the evening as I locked up, Andy would have a sheaf of quite three inches of banknotes in his broad, blunt hands. He would peel off a couple of large notes to each of the big lads and then pile them all into his large dusty Bentley and, giving me a wave, drive away.

One evening, after two months of busy Friday night shows, I remarked that I would need to get away promptly at the end of tonight's show as my mother was ill and I wanted to get home and tend to her. Andy was immediately concerned.

'Your mum – she very sick?' He looked really quite anxious.

'No, no,' I said, 'but you know how it is with the old folks. When she is unwell she won't sleep till I get in, so I want to get home and then she will relax and be comfortable.'

Andy seemed to consider this. 'Yes you are right, you must go. I hope you will find her better.'

I was really quite touched. Mum wasn't as geriatric as I was making her sound, but she had been very flu-ish throughout the previous week, and we were both concerned that it didn't turn into a protracted chest infection.

The following Friday evening Andy greeted me warmly. 'And your old mother?'

'My old mother is quite all right, thank you,' I said with what I was suddenly aware was rather a stringent tone.

'Ah – that is good,' he beamed. 'The English do not care for the parents. It is a great dishonour. You are not like that. They put them in a house with strangers. Your mother is not with strangers. That is good.'

I was too ashamed to confess that as a general rule I had as little to do with my mother as possible. And that I was now living back in my old childhood room only because I was trying to save on rent. So, based on this passive deception, Andy decided I was a good fellow and became quite chummy.

Later that evening when his sister dropped by the cinema with a small boy in tow he introduced me:

'My sister Doreen,' Andy smiled.

She too was short and round, a carbon copy of her brother. He gestured towards the toddler who was gazing round about and watching everything going on around him with a child's unblinking seriousness.

'Hah! This is Thomas; he is BBC.'

I looked rather blank at this.

'Hah! British-born Chinese!! Hah!' he barked at us all.

Doreen's face indicated that she'd heard this before. Several times before.

About three weeks later, at close to 2.45am after the last frames of that Friday's Kung-Fu double bill had passed through the projector gate, Andy was paying off his big lads from his fist full of takings when he glanced over at me.

'You come eat with us – yah?' he barked questioningly. 'Now?'

I was a bit taken aback. 'It's late, Andy – and nowhere is open.'

'Nah! We go to Chinese Town,' he scoffed. 'Good food. You ever eat good Chinese food? You come.'

It was too intriguing an offer to resist and in ten minutes more the large lads and I were all piled into the back of Andy's battered old Bentley driving very purposefully, through the dark and empty streets of south London, towards Soho. In less than half an hour we pulled up in a side street just behind Shaftesbury Avenue. It was a cool, dry night, and as we crossed the avenue the theatres were all shuttered and quiet. Even the fire station looked asleep. Not a soul stirred. I felt oddly exhilarated. Even though I was far from precisely clear as to what was to happen next, I felt perfectly safe. With these lads around me and Andy at the front of us all, I felt protected from anything short of an aerial bombing.

The whole group of six of us stepped across Shaftesbury Avenue into Gerrard Street. To my surprise and delight the whole place was humming. All the lights were on, there were folk strolling about, the restaurants and vegetable stores and Chinese supermarkets all had their lights on and were full of customers. I also perceived that by far the greater part of the people I could see appeared to be Chinese. It was like a whole secret world, with very few tourists. Andy led us up the street past many restaurants that I had seen before in my dull diurnal past but had never entered. Outside 'China City' he stopped and jerked his thumb. We wheeled round and filed in behind him. This was a very large place, spread over three floors, the sort of place that looks to have about 400 covers and is open for twenty hours a day. It appeared to be jammed to capacity with customers with not a single empty chair across the whole wide room. A floor manager saw Andy and grinned. He glanced across at the back and jerked his chin upwards. Andy immediately pointed at the stairs and leading us across the bright and crowded din of the restaurant, led us up the narrow stairs to the first floor.

Up here all the lights were ablaze also, and another large room was thrumming with activity. Here there looked to be another ten or more large round tables each seating at least ten or a dozen customers. These tables appeared to be at capacity as well. However, the floor manager walked up to us and exchanged a sentence with Andy. We followed him in single file, weaving through the tables, to a medium-sized one set against the middle of the back wall. We sat down and I was delighted to find that I had Andy seated on my left and a complete view of the whole room. Perfect.

Andy now spoke to his lads. They grunted a few replies. A sentence each. Each of them was pulling out cigarettes. Andy turned to me:

'You like Chinese food, Nick? You know Chinese food? What you want?'

Suddenly my routine lemon chicken and bean sprouts seemed very pedestrian.

'You choose,' I said, 'you know what's good.'

'Hah! Good,' he beamed.

The waiter approached with six huge plastic bound menus. Andy waved these away with a sneering smile. He spoke Cantonese rapidly to the waiter for a minute and a half, occasionally glancing at his lads who would each nod an assent. The waiter's pen flew over his note pad. He had started his third page by the time Andy had finished speaking, but he didn't seem perturbed. He turned away and disappeared through the crowded room.

By now there were cigarettes burning all round me. I tried to hide my discomfort. After all, there was an equivalent fog over every other table in the room. Fortunately there were several air-conditioner boxes set into the Styrofoam ceiling across the room.

'So you eat Chinese food before? You like?'

'Well,' I replied carefully, 'only a little, but yes, I like it very much.'

'Hah! Tonight you eat good. We all eat good. This a good place. Manager a friend of me. Good friend. From Singapore like me.'

Suddenly two very large bowls of plain boiled rice appeared as well as a bottle of Johnny Walker Black Label whisky. And two teapots. And six small tea bowls. And six dimpled Duralex French drinking tumblers. And a forest of cream-coloured plastic sticks. Andy passed all round busily making sure I had a glass and a cup and then, handing me a pair of the sticks, he frowned earnestly.

'You know chopsticks, Nick? You need fork and knife?' He was half-turned towards the retreating waiter already.

'No,' I said, 'I know how to use chopsticks.'

Oddly, this was true. My mother had first met Chinese cuisine during her time in South Africa years before in the early 1950s when there had been no alternative offered and so, as her sons grew up in London, she had taught us all from a young age. Andy was very pleased at this.

'Ah. I thought so. You are educated, I'm sure,' he smiled.

'No, but my mum took all her children out to eat and we liked Chinese food. So she taught us.'

'Exactly. You are educated,' insisted Andy, unscrewing the whisky bottle and pouring a generous slug of neat Scotch into my tumbler.

He poured round the table, then put the bottle back down in the middle. Barely a third remained. He raised his glass and proposed a toast. The others all raised their glasses. Andy swallowed his at a gulp. The others took a good slurp each but didn't empty their glasses. I barely sipped at mine and put it down.

There then arrived severally many mysteries: creamy white folds of mysterious deliciousness that I hoped might be steamed dumplings, on another plate pieces of a very dark meat in a thick gravy with chopped onions and beans floating next to it, on another a whole filleted sea bass with the plate decorated with the fish's head at one end and its tail at the other, yet another plate on which were some bright yellow fragments of wizened looking gristle. Also another two pots of tea. All these, smelling utterly delightful, were placed on the turntable in the table centre. Andy gestured and the lads began to swing the turntable and to help themselves liberally. As soon as everyone had a full bowl they also lit a fresh cigarette each and refilled their whisky glasses. So now eating and smoking and drinking gustily all at once, everyone tucked in. I put some rice in my bowl and helped myself to some of the pretty sea bass. There were chillies in the sauce but the effect was not unpleasantly hot. The warmth was actually in the mouth rather than in the throat and belly, as with a curry. A novel and pleasing difference. Next, I tried the plate of dark coloured meat – this turned out to be braised and marinated lamb in shaved slices, the thick gravy very mildly spiced also.

Andy and the lads didn't talk much at first. In the cheery hubbub of that nocturnal palace, we six were quietly satiating some serious post-work hunger. The food was as delicious and plentiful as it was filling, so we were all happy. In about twenty-five minutes we were all beginning to come up for air. I noticed that all the glasses, save mine, were empty, as was the whisky bottle. The teapots were being replenished every ten minutes or so. As they slowed up the big lads began to chat steadily one to another, but rarely to Andy. They would occasionally raise an eyebrow towards me as they replaced a dish or as they considered the smaller remaining portions on the table. As often as I could I nodded a yes. The only plate I felt unwilling to revisit was the one with the yellow fragments. It had been gristle indeed, and I had not enjoyed chewing and swallowing even the small amount I'd taken of something so evidently pointless and nasty.

Andy looked round the room as he lit what had to be his fourth cigarette.

'You like your food?' He suddenly caught my eye as he gazed around.

'Oh yes, very much,' I replied truthfully. 'So many things I never ate before. What is the yellow…' Andy smiled and cut me off.

'Very delicious, no? Is chicken feet. Lucky food. Very nice. Very special here.'

I smiled my understanding and hoped that he hadn't noticed how little I'd eaten of this particular delicacy.

Suddenly Andy straightened up in his chair, his eyes moving away from me. I noticed his attention and followed his gaze. The big lads looked as well, but immediately turned back to smoking and drinking quietly amongst themselves. Andy remained watchful as he smoked. He was quiet but concentrating. I had seen his friend the manager from the floor below pass by once or twice, but now I noticed that when he did there was usually a waiter or two behind him bearing large trays of food. These all went to a very large table in the opposite corner. At the table that would easily have taken ten more people sat only two men, both in dark suits. They sat almost shoulder to shoulder, but not in a posture that suggested intimacy. They each had a cigarette in hand and, at their elbows, a bottle of Scotch each. The table, from what I could see, appeared to be groaning with food. There were nine or eleven very elaborate dishes of all kinds crammed onto the table in front of these two. All this bounty they resolutely ignored as they spoke earnestly to each other.

Andy saw me looking and hissed to me closely,

'Watch very quietly. Big men. Manager is friend of me. He is giving present to Big Men. Important business. Watch very quietly.'

Suddenly I noticed that at the two adjoining tables on either side of each of the big men were seated two or three further men in suits, each group sitting so they had a clear line of sight of the other secondary group, whilst yet remaining in the protective shadow of their own primary big man. Clearly these fellows had seen as many gangster movies as I had and knew how to conduct themselves properly. It was all as fascinating as it was mildly alarming. Andy confirmed to me that the discussion going on across the room probably did not concern the restaurant itself. Rather, this was probably a business meeting between senior members of rival gangs that controlled loan sharking and private gambling clubs and some parts of the local sex trade in the surrounding area and that while Andy's friend would certainly be paying tax to one of the men, this evening he was merely paying a suitably lavish tribute to both. I ate dinner with Andy and his lads about half a dozen times through the rest of that year, but I never again witnessed anything like that groaning table and those sombre smoking men.

Over time I did become increasingly aware of more of the nocturnal variations of the Gerrard Street habitat, however. In the daytime in the early 1980s Gerrard Street was the centre of the Chinese business community of London, the streets around it also filled with restaurants and fish markets and grocery stores of the kind that concentrated on exotic fruits and vegetables which, when labelled at all, were labelled in Chinese or, more occasionally, Hindi characters. Many of the customers would be from China or South-East Asia. In the daytime there would be the more general type of tourist, but at night these were rare. Also the shoppers bought far more at night. They would be re-supplying their own Chinese restaurants and take-away businesses in the outer suburbs. Nowadays this has all evolved considerably. The big supermarkets in Gerrard Street are still trading. But now there are large-scale Asian cash-and-carry suppliers all round London's orbital roads and I have no doubt that most of the ordering is done online. But back in the eighties we were all at an earlier stage of development.

At night in Chinatown one was much more aware of the rather unwelcoming and shabby doors at the bottom of stairwells that led off the street. These were often explicitly unwelcome, bearing messages such as 'Chinese Only' in wobbly capitals or instead, below a few Chinese characters: 'Chinese Social Club. Privat. Pleese keep out'. These were the gambling clubs and mah-jong parlours where legend had it the waiters and porters of the area went to gamble away their wages to the local tong gangs. There was prostitution too, but it was always, it seemed to me, rather more discreet than on the other side of Shaftesbury Avenue. Here the women were in the clubs rather than on the streets. Also, the Soho gay scene had not developed yet quite the established public character it now has, and so was less obvious on this south-eastern side of the Avenue.

The effects of those late suppers with Andy are still with me. They established my preference for the spicier Hunan and Szechuan styles of Chinese food and gave me my meagre knowledge of it that I would later develop on annual visits to New York where this sub-genre of Chinese food was already better established. In London, for a decade or more afterwards, I felt very confident of my judgement of the particular virtues of specific restaurants throughout the Chinatown area. In those days I even shopped in the frozen-food sections of the Lisle and Gerrard Street grocery shops, as well as equipping myself with steaming baskets and a cheap wok and a chef's chopper all rather before they became conventional wedding gifts in all the Oxford Street department stores.

But running the cinema in Tooting was not all nocturnal orgies of Asiatic gastronomy. On the home turf there was enough to contend with. I mentioned earlier that Andy's clientele for his Friday night Kung-Fu shows was almost exclusively young, male and Black. This derived logically from the proximity of Tooting to Brixton. In Brixton many, but by no means all, of the local residents share a Caribbean heritage. Indeed Brixton has been one of the principal areas of Black British residency since the end of the Second World War. Many people and their businesses thrive there but too many suffer the consequences of the poisonous social compound of joblessness, under-skilling, poverty, substance abuse, street crime, and intermittent neglect by the higher powers. This protracted voiceless suffering has the ultimate consequence, in London as elsewhere in the world, of erupting into brief periods of explosive mass criminality.

In the spring of 1981 one such moment occurred. The police in the area had wide powers to stop and search any individual whom they had 'reasonable suspicion to believe' was carrying drugs or weapons. The 'sus' law, from the point of view of many of the residents, amounted to systematic and routine public harassment and humiliation on a daily basis. In this climate any infraction by either party would be inflamed by rumour and gossip into a provocation for further transgression on both sides.

The 'Brixton Riots', as they have become known historically, were more accurately a series of running street battles between loose confederations of mainly, but by no means exclusively, local Black youths who attacked the police wherever they could and pillaged and burned local businesses the while. It was a bad time for everyone. It took the police the best part of a week to organise an effective response and to re-take firm control of the streets in the area. For the local lads of Tooting, both White and Black, this was mainly a very exciting spectacle. There was noise and danger and moderate risk and a sense of retributive street justice that was thoroughly intoxicating for some.

In the Tooting Street where the lowly Classic Cinema stood nothing particularly out of the ordinary occurred, but the sense of potential threat was very real, especially when young former customers would come running into the foyer during the afternoon and shout breathlessly something like, 'Is me mate Darren in there?' before running away again, not even staying for an answer. Others would occasionally push into the hall, but when they saw that all was comparatively quiet they would soon leave.

Oddly, but perhaps logically, these very regular interruptions rarely occurred after nightfall. Perhaps by then people had already met up and made their arrangements to go down to the 'Front Line', as the streets a little north of Electric Avenue was known in those alarming few days. Such disruptions were exasperating even for me, as indeed they would be for anyone in a position of responsibility but who has really no effective power at all.

For George, the doorman at the Classic Tooting, the disruptions were far more deeply disturbing. There had always been a steady amount of rowdyism and attempts to bunk in at any and all shows by young local lads. The presence of George was meant to discourage this. He was a big man, very gentle really, but he was a local 'face' and so commanded some respect. However, he had a very clear sense that the respect which he so judiciously guarded had accrued to him personally rather than to his position as public greeter, guide, bouncer, porter and general all-round interventionist at the local flea-pit cinema.

He was therefore disinclined to wear any uniform of any kind, nor to be seen to do any manual lifting once the hall was open. I told him it would be illegal for him to work at the cinema without being clearly identified as a staff member. We agreed that he would wear plain, dark shirt and trousers and a name badge. Privately regretting the badge, he later added a short scarf to his costume, the ends of which he contrived always to accidently drape over the offending nameplate. Whenever I pointed this sartorial oddity out to him, he would look nonplussed then flick the end of the little tartan scarf over his shoulder and smile at me gently. In that gesture he always put me in mind of Rupert Bear, irresistibly. But so long as his sense of himself was not likely to be compromised, George would do whatever I asked of him. Within reason. His reason, of course.

George's dilemma was really that he lived close by; the local streets were where he was known in the rest of his daily life, and so any challenge to his position at the cinema was part of the wider realm of that life. He was very displeased with thieves who stole things from other patrons or strangers who tried to bunk in. With lads he knew he would try to be persuasive – they had to pay to enter, it was the right thing to do, blades were not allowed, such items would only escalate any potential disagreement, they would have to give up the blade or leave.

But George was fatally prone to making his own private compromises with folk he knew – if three paid, the fourth could come in free or, with a full house, if they gave him cigarettes they could sit on the auditorium steps in the dark. To some of this I turned a blind eye, believing that I was employing someone who otherwise had precious few employable skills, and that his routine presence was also a visible public investment in the immediate community, linking us to the passers-by. And he did not get flustered in ordinary situations of argy-bargy – he would try to defuse any clash diplomatically but would unhesitatingly manhandle anyone who was impolite.

With the sudden breakdown of law in the wider world just beyond the cinema, George was faced with a new challenge. Some people would argue more aggressively now in any situation whatsoever, almost immediately threatening violence if they were not immediately granted admission, no matter that they were already drunk or high or just wildly over-excited. Sometimes a shouting row would develop out of something absurd like a sudden demand that George immediately buy the cartons of cigarettes the panting young salesman had suddenly to hand. If George refused and asked the young man to take his trade outside it could well develop into shouts, threats, a challenge.

One afternoon, almost a week after several nights of disturbance in the streets south of us were over, I walked through the lobby on an errand and saw the backs of three lads pushing out into the street, each carrying four or so medium-sized cardboard boxes. Then I saw that our chest freezer that lived at the back of the lobby had had its locks and bolts forced open and so about twenty cases of frozen cinema hotdogs were now disappearing up the street. I yelled for George, who trundled up quickly enough from the back of the inner dark. I sent him off in pursuit. He jogged out along the street.

As he reached the corner of the road one lad looked back and bellowed at George,

'George you cunt, I seed you fuckin' nickin' 'em trainers las' week you wanker yah!' and then ran on.

George, wearing his smart new shoes, walked slowly back to the cinema doors. I ducked back inside and made myself busy trying to put the top lock-plates back onto the almost empty freezer. I mimed having heard not a word. George's face was a picture of angry bewilderment.

In as much as he should have been in the empty vestibule of the cinema at that hour and would then have prevented, in all probability, this absurd, expensive and, for me, inconvenient crime, he'd failed in his job. Further he'd been exposed to a public challenge because of that job – which for all I knew was utterly untrue – and he now had to resolve the employee side of that same challenge with me. I decided that I would make no reference to his new trainers in any sense, just reprimand him mildly for his lapse of attention to duty. To be fair to George a cinema foyer on a mid-week afternoon is not a place you might expect a passing criminal to think a good spot to pick up valuables worth stealing, and if there were any on the premises worth the risk they'd be far more likely to be found in the pockets and bags of the few customers sitting in the dark inside, which is where George had been anyway. So I spoke to him firmly about the need to be more vigilant to which he assented glumly.

A week later, on another afternoon, I was doing paperwork in my office at the back of the house and heard someone trying to rattle free the bolts of the emergency side door. This was a more determined trial than was usual so I put down my pen and walked through to the dark auditorium to see exactly what was happening. I was just in time to see George holding open the emergency exit door and pocketing a coin from each figure as they slipped in past him.

I sacked him that day, but with a heavy heart. I now had no in-house security whatever, and I had made at least a tacit enemy of a local face who had friends. But, in truth, nothing more happened with respect to George and the local lads just misbehaved in and around the premises as ever but were no worse than before. However, I was heartily glad when the opportunity to move on finally arrived. I was feeling very unsafe, the already modest takings had declined further after the riots, as had much of the general trade in the immediate area, and I was now routinely on anti-depressants supplied by my sympathetic doctor because of the ludicrous fret of it all. Mr Brown, the bullying ignoramus of a regional manager, advised that a slot had opened up in Hampstead in north-west London. The manager there needed an assistant. Immediately. There would be a small salary increment. It could have been viewed as a demotion, in as much as I was moving from a manager to an assistant manager position, but I was so ready to leave the grimy purlieus of south London for pastures new in the north that this change of status worried me not a whit.

The Classic 123, Pond Street, Hampstead with the Royal Free Hospital behind, 1979

Opened in August 1914 as the Hampstead Picture Playhouse, this cinema originally had seating for 1,500. It was closed for much of the Second World War. In 1965 it was purchased by the Classic Cinemas chain which modernised the exterior in 1968 and converted it to a triple screen operation in 1978. The Cannon Group took over in 1985. Six years later it became the MGM and in 1995 Virgin took control but it was named ABC in the years prior to its closure in late 2000. Following the building's demolition in 2003, a food store with flats above was built on the site.

Cinema Theatre Association Archive

The Classic Cinema, Hampstead Autumn 1981

Hampstead turned out to be a markedly different sort of proposition to Tooting. Where the Classic Tooting had been an utterly faded 790-seater single hall with an elderly projectionist and leaking toilets, the Classic Hampstead was a thriving triplex hall sited at the crossroads of a busy local shopping area, adjoining a famous teaching hospital.

This cinema had three halls, the largest of which had once been the former raised circle seating area back when the cinema had been a single grand auditorium. On the ground floor were now two smaller halls in the area that had formerly been the stalls, cut in half by a dividing wall.

There were two projection suites, one to serve the larger upper auditorium that seated around 260, and another joint-projection suite to serve the two lower halls that seated about 190 and 188 in the other. This was a classic mid-seventies division and conversion of a traditional single auditorium: the dividing walls were made of barely soundproofed breeze-block. With a pair of new fire doors for each hall and the simple addition of new style 'cake-stand' projectors, the job was considered done.

The impetus behind this trend towards the conversion of almost all of the old single halls was entirely economically driven. As mass audiences had continued to decline relentlessly every year through the post-war decades, the owners of the big cinema chains had adapted nearly all their halls in this or a very similar way. The others they sold off. There were several clear commercial advantages to the chains in this procedure. With three halls instead of one they could rent three titles instead of one, thus ensuring that they could sell more tickets to more films and so have more customers at any time of the day. It also gave them some flexibility of trade. Typically the big new release of the week would open in the larger hall and then, in the second or third week of its run, as attendances dropped off, be moved to one of the smaller halls. In some localities it was also possible to experiment, ever so very modestly, with foreign titles. Perhaps last year's foreign Oscar winner or some similarly safe title might be tried out in the local Screen 3. Owners would hope to pick up some business on the back of a local ethnic interest at least as much as from the media campaign carefully planned nationally by the distributor – i.e. big spreads in the weekend and Sunday papers supported by media interviews.

In as much as more films played at the local cinema, and that individual titles could remain available for a little longer for that local viewer to catch up with, there were some real gains for the consumer. But the consequence of poor structural maintenance, insensitive conversions with cheap materials and minimal expenditure on decorative maintenance, meant that over time all the halls became, slowly and steadily, shabbier and shabbier. The 'glamour of the cinema' is still much evoked in any convenient context by cinema's promoters on every feasible occasion but, in the 1970s and 80s, the reality of cinema-going at the provincial sites of the national chains was, all too often, draughty, cold halls, evil-smelling toilets, faded and shabby curtains and drapes, dead bulbs in light fixtures, worn carpeting, and grotesquely over-priced and grubby concession stands at which barely trained teenage staff served lamentable coffee and chemical ice-cream. With the steady rise of alternative ways to watch films through all these years, it's a testament to the power of advertising and human habit that cinemas even today have hung on as long as they have.

As I approached the Hampstead cinema, in that autumn of 1981 for the very first time, I saw that its marquee proclaimed the three titles it was currently screening *10 / Meatballs / Escape from Alcatraz*. I was charmed. As ever, the cinema itself was rather worn at the edges, the seats were saggy, the carpeting had been replaced only in the essential areas, and the curtains were grubby. The long foyer and the sales area that faced the four pairs of glass doors was very draughty on all but the warmest days. But with the right titles trade was always brisk.

It transpired that the manager, Chris Churchill, had lost his assistant manager some three weeks previously to a burger franchise and so had been working solo for twenty-one days or more. The comic-sounding combination of titles on the marquee outside had been a very big draw for the public; being a popular rom-com, a teen gross-out satire, and a jail-break thriller respectively, so the site was doing capacity business in all halls at all the later showings and was expected to continue this welcome trend for a few weeks at least.

Therefore Chris, as well as his crew, were all rather feeling the strain. Chris was a man both gaunt and tall, his thin face, sunken eyes and prematurely greying beard suggesting a much older man than he in fact was. He was intelligent and clearly living on his nerves. He was sallow, rumpled, and smoked constantly. The backs of his hands were thickly veined, his fingers were long and thin and yellow from nicotine. Yet he ran a good ship and seemed to be respected by most of the staff. A few of them were very fond of him, and when quieter times arrived, I was to see why. He could be inventively droll and was given to unexpected moments of dry whimsy.

But right now Chris had to induct me into the essential procedures of operating a fast moving and complex specialist retail operation which was quite unlike the relative backwater where I had been vegetating for nearly half a year. Here there was a full-time permanent staff of about ten, including the three projectionists, and another near dozen part-timers who came in to do evening and weekend shifts on demand. I had to learn their names, their duties, their actual individual capacities and weaknesses immediately. I also had to learn the security procedures, the fire drills, the money handling routines, the staffing and re-stocking cycles for the sales areas as well as all the paperwork relating to all of these. This was still the era when most of the staff expected to be paid in cash on a weekly basis. So later I would have to learn the wage preparation procedures, the paying out and the detailed record-keeping for this. In truth, I had already done much of this in one way or another on different sites. But Hampstead was a far larger cog in the Classic Cinemas commercial machine than I was familiar with, so there was much to get right and very little room for error. It was all a very far cry from the days of Dad's quiet antiquarian bookshop, where I had simply turned the sign on the front door to 'Closed', dropped the day's takings into a bank bag, thrown the bag into the safe, locked it, turned off all the lights, locked the shop door and strolled off to my bed.

By contrast, this big untidy place was exhilarating. There is a definite gratification to be had from operating a cinema full of smiling customers. At its best it's a bit like hosting a successful party: you are run off your feet, you're not sure if you have enough supplies of everything, but you get a contact high from being surrounded by cheery, contented faces. They will probably spend a little more money, and they are a little more likely to come back to your cinema if they sense that they've enjoyed both the film and the cinema in which they saw it.

Of course, it is always precisely at these busy times that the cinema's infrastructure strains to cope – for example the toilets block up or a projector bulb blows or a gang of lads, unwilling to pay, try to pry open each of the fire doors from the street. In addition, this is always the moment when, just as you are at last admitting the queue that has been waiting patiently for half an hour, earlier patrons will come running up demanding that you immediately help them find their car keys or their umbrella which they're convinced they've left on the floor of the hall. Equally it's not a good moment for five customers in a row to expect change from a £50 note or a light bulb to choose to fail inside an emergency exit sign.

All of these events happened in the next three weeks, I seem to remember, and some of them more than once. I believe my basic wage was now about £85 a week, and I think I earned it. Hampstead also had late shows on Friday and Saturday nights. Thankfully these were only single titles, not the exhausting double bills of the Pullman and Screen on the Green days. But it still meant finishing at around 1.45am which is a long while after an 11.00am start, especially if the house has been busy through most of the day. Pacing yourself was important. I have to admit I rather took to drink to get through the hours: I would easily get through an entire large-size bottle of Lucozade in a single evening.

The weekend late shows came always with moments of drama. There was the time Trevor and Rex, the two sombre West Indian doormen, came to me at the very end of a long Friday night to tell me that there were two dead girls upstairs in Screen 1. I was shutting the safe in the office, planning on getting home quickly to watch the Truffaut film I hoped my new-fangled VHS machine would have recorded for me. The two of them stood there, beside each other, their faces both stiff with alarm and misery.

'Come again?' I asked faintly.

'Day's two girls in Screen 1. Day's dead, I'm t'inkin,' said Rex as they both looked at me.

'Well, let's go see,' I said, hoping my rising sense of horror and panic was not over-apparent.

And down the office back stairs we tumbled, across the dark and locked foyer and up to Screen 1. The other staff had all left. Trevor and Rex's last routine duty was to do the final security check, that is, to walk all round each auditorium, checking for smouldering cigarettes or broken glass or lost property and also to check the toilets one last time, for damage or dozing patrons. We stepped into the back of Screen 1 and I turned on the double pair of 200-watt bulbs of the cleaner's lights, flooding the whole space with a harsh raw overhead glare. The hall looked bleak, dingy and dirty. Two rows in from the back, there was indeed a pair of very tousled heads leaning against each other. I approached from the rear.

'Hello!' I shouted. 'Time to go home. The show's over.'

The two heads did not move. I was now standing behind them. I could see a very pale youngish ear, with a hooped earing. I put out a hand and prodded gently.

'Hello!' I repeated. I was becoming hot with alarm. I walked quickly round to stand in front.

They were two teenaged girls, one dark, one fair. They were both the colour of milk. I was very frightened now. The lads were watching me.

'Day's dead, ain't day?' said Rex again, with real sorrow.

Almost holding my breath, I leaned very close up to the nearest of the two and put my ear to her mouth. 'Shush!' I croaked.

I could smell alcohol. I put my ear against her face and I thought I could hear the faintest wheeze of exhalation. They were both pale and cold but they were not stiff and they were both breathing, albeit very faintly. Now I took the blonde one gently by the shoulders and shook her. She complained in a slurred, soft moan.

'They're not dead, guys,' I said with as much relief as they, 'these young ladies are just dead drunk, I think.'

I was a bit cross now. This was just teenage stupidity. But they were alarmingly insensible, even for drunks. I poked at them again and shouted again. No response whatever. Both flopped over when I pushed at them, as pliable as mannequins. Not even a drunk's groan of discomfort this time. They weren't shamming, their faces were too slack, but they were out stone cold. But it was more than drunkenness, surely? I stepped back a pace and straightened up to tell the chaps to wait while I went to the office to use the phone to call for an ambulance. Then, as I looked down again at the inert pair of bodies, I spied two or three little white containers under the seats. I could see immediately that they were prescription pill bottles. I scooped one up. It was quite empty. The polysyllabic label meant nothing to me. But I knew what to do.

'Rex, Trevor – these ladies are not dead. They're breathing. They've taken pills. The Royal Free Hospital is right next door. It's Friday night and the ambulances will be very busy. If I call for an ambulance it will take at least fifteen minutes. Let's carry these two ladies across to the A&E and put them in front of the doctors right now.'

I reached down, picked up the other two pill bottles and put them in my pocket. Trevor hoisted one lady onto his shoulders and Rex the other. I pushed open the fire doors and led the way down the steep back stairs and so out into the lamp-lit street.

The two lads carried their rag doll apiece out into the night without any apparent effort. We quickly walked the fifty yards, under the sodium glow of the streetlights, to the hospital emergency entrance. It was the usual scene from Dante within. Bloodied children with glass in their hair, men with faces swollen from pub fights, wailing babies in the arms of panicked parents. Harsh lights, organised confusion, misery. Leading my caravan,

I marched up to the first stethoscope I could see. I stood up in front of him trying to look commanding.

'These two ladies – I think they've taken a lot of drugs. I don't know what. I've brought them from the cinema next door. I'm leaving them here with you… These were under their feet – here,' I said firmly as I dropped into his palm the three little bottles I was holding and then gestured to the lads to deposit their loads on the nearest pair of vacant chairs.

I immediately turned and walked to the door with Trevor and Rex close behind me. Outside I felt a lot better. Trevor and Rex were standing up straight too, looking very relieved.

'Time to go home, gentlemen,' said I. 'Many thanks. I needed your help tonight, so thank you both again.'

They looked at each other and then at me and then grinned huge grins of relief.

'Ah needs me one col' one for sure now,' said Trevor.

I smiled back. 'The pubs are long shut – but you'll be having one indoors, no?' I said.

Trevor smiled at me. 'Ah knows a place still be open.'

'Oh, naturally.'

They both chuckled and walked softly away to Trevor's very dirty van. By the time I'd locked up the cinema again and got my taxi home I was very tired. Slumped in front of the TV I barely made it through the titles of Truffaut's *Anne and Muriel* before I was ready for bed.

I think I hinted earlier that living back in my childhood room, along the corridor from my mum, was not the perfect domestic arrangement that Chinese Andy might have supposed. By the time I had been at the Hampstead cinema a week I had moved out of home once more and taken a rented room in a flat in West London. I was a mortgage tenant. Again. Martha's flat I had found through a specialist rental agency. The furnished room she offered in her snug little apartment was very small indeed. But I could afford it, it was clean, and she was friendly. The flat was the whole top floor of what had once been a very large Victorian family home. There was a lounge full of large-format art books lounging aslant on tousled shelves, with keepsakes and menu cards and framed citations and trinkets sprinkled lushly over all the side tables and all along the window shelves. On the outside ledges of the windows were verdant window-boxes, evidently tended with care. There was a modest but well-planned kitchen, crammed with culinary kit, a larger bedroom with an en-suite bathroom for Martha, a guest bathroom adjoining the lounge, and my little mouse hole of a room at the far end of the corridor. It always felt warm in that flat, and well-designed skylights meant there could be air and light at any time. Being up under the eaves the ceilings were low throughout, but the effect was homely. Having worked in television almost all her life she seemed to feel some mild sympathy for the idea of having a dormant assistant cinema manager in her spare bedroom snoring through the early mornings.

Martha was one of a style of lady I had not met before, though I was soon to learn that there were many like her. She had been closely involved with the birth of commercial television in England. She had been a personal assistant to a succession of the new commercial TV executives, who had evolved out of some of the people who had formerly worked at the top end of advertising. These were both contiguous worlds of big money and high-stakes chance-taking. The commercial broadcasters in Britain have always seen themselves as far more down-to-earth and commercially realistic than their powerful rival, the BBC.

In the mid-1950s, when commercial TV broadcasting began in Britain, this mind-set was somewhat justified, in that the BBC had a government-supported monopoly of the radio airwaves as well as the only national TV channel. The BBC was therefore the default source for news, for big sporting events, for high- and low-brow entertainment. The new commercial and regional TV channels had to adopt a sort of Barnum & Bailey rationale: 'Never under-estimate the public's taste' was their credo. They bought in lots of popular American western shows and cop shows; they commissioned new British variants of these from clever, hungry writers and dressed them with new British TV stars. On the commercial channel there were more quiz shows – often franchised from American models – and more popular music shows. I remember being addicted to the cartoon shows on the ITV channel in the later part of my childhood. The adventures of 'Popeye the Sailor Man' seemed livelier than the adventures of 'Bill & Ben the flower-pot men' on the other side of the TV dial.

So Martha had worked for years in the racier world of the anti-Beeb, in the days when there had been only two TV channels, and all was to play for. Of course, then as now, the essential difference between the two business models was that the BBC received an income from the sale of television licences to the general public (its own government-permitted tax upon the viewing public) where the commercial stations, the 'other side', were dependent on the sale of advertising time slots between the programmes. Thus they were, and remain today, effectively indistinguishable from the traditional American network model. And these new British commercial channels resented this fundamental difference of funding, perceived back then as an unfair advantage. They do still.

Martha was not now young, but she was impressively trim. She was a gym-going, yoga-class-taking, yoghurt-eating metropolitan dweller to her very polished fingers' ends. Her honey blonde hair was expensively coloured and cut and her clothes always fitted her well. She was relaxed in male company and drank spirits and smoked with the best of them. She could manage a good dirty laugh when sufficiently relaxed. I suspect other women had always regarded her carefully.

Martha's version of her history was that she had never married, but in her later working years had been the very personal assistant to one of the topmost men from the founding days of commercial television. He had been one of those high-flyers who had ultimately been awarded, by a slightly dazzled leftist Prime Minister, a knighthood as the final triumph of a very bitterly fought professional career in the new world of television development. This commercial paragon had retired and then immediately died, utterly unexpectedly, from a massive stroke the minute he stepped off the commercial battlefield. Perhaps Martha had hoped that she would escape with her prize, having detached him from the wife he had barely tolerated for years and years as well as the grown children he so despaired of, to some sunnier shore. But instead she was now the detached one, living in a smallish flat, filled with media awards and signed menus as memory markers, watering her window boxes.

But Martha was not alone. There was Ray. Ray was very charming and nearing his forties, but very fit indeed. He was tanned with a wide, blue-eyed smile and an engaging laugh. He was very conversational, very quick on the uptake. Ray and a partner loaned fleets of cars to companies and individuals. A system of long-term rental: a limousine firm, for example, would rent their cars from Ray, and then replace them every year. I suspect the terms could be adjusted so that insurance and tax overheads were significantly reduced. Ray indicated he was doing very well, and, looking back, his sense of commercial timing was perfect: the roaring 1980s were just emerging – all cocaine on the stock market floors and bloated hedge fund managers spending their expense accounts on ferrying favoured clients, via private jets, to Paris brothels. There was a very great deal of discretionary spending in certain areas of London life. Ray spoke with a brisk Cockney confidence, like Michael Caine, and, also like Michael Caine, favoured many of the celebrity restaurants.

One evening, soon after I had moved in, Martha invited me to join the two of them when they went to a favourite haunt of theirs. Martha suggested I might want to dress up as this was to be a bit of an outing. 'Do you have something…?' she asked in that solicitous tone that well-dressed women usually use for each other. I said that I thought that I did. Come the evening Martha looked very soignée, in a belted wrap-around of grey cashmere, with gold at her neck and ears. Ray wore a wide-lapelled closely tailored evening jacket in midnight blue that fitted him like a young roebuck's skin. He looked like a junior adjutant in a fashionable infantry regiment, now out of uniform but dressed for his sister's engagement party. I wore my only suit, an Italian-cut double-breasted two piece in a dark grey pinstripe, with front pleats and turn-ups on the trousers. (Bought at an end-of-season sale for a bargain price the year before, it was to serve me well through a number of weddings and job interviews in the next few years.)

The special place that they were so fond of turned out to be a small private casino in a series of adjoining basements under the Kings Road, Chelsea. A long narrow room, with a dozen air-conditioning units in the ceiling, very plush, all gilt candelabra and red velvet sofas, with 'tasteful' oils of modern nudes hanging along the walls. There was a fair bit of noise in this non-gaming area of the sequence of rooms: the kind of near hysterical over-bright chatter that swims round you at a gallery opening or a first-night theatre after-party. More than a few of the same people too, I thought. But perhaps not entirely, as a fair number of the crowd were very silvered, and there were a lot of leathery throats on view. Many people were clustered along the walnut panelled bar, others were browsing on the food laid out on a long table. This consisted of hot entrées served under warm lids, with big bowls of salad on the side. There were large jugs of orange juice also, and though chilled, it was canned. The swirling din of this dining and drinking room actually proved more diverting to me than the sombre gaming room next door.

This was nearly half as large again as the socialising room, but the light level was halved. Over the green and gold roulette tables hung a fug of smoke, and around them were grey faces all concentrating hard. Voices were muted, mouths were stiff, eyes were lowered. The age disparities were more marked here. Some women played alone, but it was mostly men who gambled, and many had companions at their elbows who were younger than themselves, sometimes by several decades. No one seemed ever to smile, no-one seemed ever to want to look away from the vortex of the roulette wheel or, over at the blackjack tables, to look up from their cards. The tension in here was all adrenaline-based, not sexual at all. And the faces were, so often, exactly the faces that Rowlandson and Gillray had drawn two hundred years ago. The wigs had gone, and there were more faces that would have been read as foreign and exotic in 18th century London, but those were the only differences I could see.

After I had watched Ray and Martha for half an hour or so at the roulette table I moved back to the hospitality room. Here customers paid for any alcoholic drink, though the food was available for all. The earlier covered dishes had all disappeared to be replaced with fresh ones smelling of bacon and sausage and grilled tomatoes. There were assorted pretty rolls piled in baskets at each end of the table. The theme, clearly, was breakfast. I drank about a pint and a half of the not-so-nice orange juice, and then helped myself to a large helping of scrambled eggs and smoked salmon and toast. After a mug or two of coffee I was starting to feel at least rewarded for this odd evening. In another hour or so Ray and Martha appeared looking rather drawn and, scarcely speaking, indicated it was time to go home immediately. I gestured towards the breakfast beano at their elbows, while wiping crumbs from my face, but they shook their heads. Outside in the cool of the very early summer morning we climbed into Ray's black Rover and drove rapidly northwest through the nearly deserted streets, towards Latimer Road. We climbed the stairs silently to the flat and whispered our goodnights on the landing. I fell onto my little cot of a bed and awoke some seven hours later.

Though they did ask me again at least once they never pressed me, and I never socialised with them again outside the house. Perhaps I had seemed dull; certainly I had enjoyed myself only tangentially. I love spending money, and too often do so unwisely, but actually throwing it away is not something I can do easily. Ray and Martha did seem happy in each other's company – they would often reappear in the kitchen doorway side by side, fresh from some outing together, as I was eating a midnight meal having finished a day's work at the Hampstead cinema. Coffees or cognacs would be made or offered and, very occasionally, we would all watch something together on her little telly. My VHS recorder, which I had wired up to Martha's TV, was a mild novelty back then, meaning that she was always doubly pleased if I had taped something for her. Martha was a decent enough landlady, not minding my habit of sleeping through the mornings and then breakfasting at 10.00am before heading off to work each day. Typically, at the end of a working day, I fell back through the door at close to midnight. I would wash my face, make myself something to eat, and then watch an hour or so of telly before turning off the lights at 2.00am.

Hampstead was a busy cinema and there was a lot to do. Chris, my new boss, was not a quiet man. With his smoking, his thin wrists and his intermittent beard (he would grow it, then shave it off, grow it again, then shave it off again about three times in a sort of annual cycle) he was a good teacher, but I don't think I was ever more than an average student. He did tutor me in all the book-keeping I needed and the rather more complex matter of wages preparation – involving the use of government tax tables for all the deductions – as well as the equally complex pattern of overtime payments for the projectionists. Then we had to prepare and send off the cinema's programme timetable details to all the local papers before noon every Monday. There was, too, a weekly timetable to prepare of the schedule of the actual auditorium screening times. This was essential, amongst other things, for getting the usherettes from one hall to the next so that there were enough ladies on hand to get people seated at the start of each crowded weekend house. There was stock reordering for the sales area as well as a daily plan for shifting stock from the various storerooms to the sales area before opening up. If we ever had to do a mid-evening restock this could be complicated with the need for diverted manpower, security keys, the opening and closing of locked fridges or secure cigarette cupboards and the possible (very temporary) blocking of fire corridors or exits. I had a lot to learn. But what was at least as important, and more complicated to work out, was the patterns within the staff. Who could be completely relied upon to do exactly what you asked of them? Who would do only the minimum they could get away with? Which of the usherettes could be trusted not to wander off for a smoke during a quiet moment? Which of the doormen could be trusted not to make passes at every female member of staff, as a matter of incorrigible habit, thereby causing offence in too many cases?

Perhaps most subtle of all was knowing which people to set in teams to work together. Some people, I found, only worked efficiently if teamed with their friends. Others were more flexible but could only work very specific hours because of child-care or other domestic issues outside the cinema. It seemed to me fortunate that there appeared to be a small but effectively inexhaustible cadre of older ladies everywhere who will work for years and years at the same local cinema, watching the managers come and go down the years who, in some senses, can be the mainstay of that particular operation. Their slot suits them, they understand their tasks, and provided any changes of costume, of teamwork, of routine, of responsibility are kept to a minimum, they will adjust and work loyally and helpfully for years. Just a little kindness – even just remembering to ask after a favourite granddaughter once in a month – will ensure a mild smile and prompt arrival at work for the start of a shift almost in perpetuity.

At the other end of the scale are youngsters who may display every degree of fecklessness and vagary. They don't like the uniform, so they lose bits of it, they come to work late or constantly petition to leave early. Commonly, the most disruptive aspect of staff behaviour was the love affairs. Some of the young lads would lose no opportunity to lay siege to the young females who coped with this with all the varied skills women have historically always used to manage such male behaviour. When the friendships flourished and the two people concerned had also managed to retain the friendship of others on the staff, then all would usually go well. The presence of a contented pair can even have a small but leavening effect on the mood of the place as a whole. But when the relationship founders for any reason whatever, then the wailing and the gnashing of teeth, the sobbing of female pairs in corridors, the male growling, cigarette stubbing, muttering on the forecourt, the damp eyes, the faces of gloom and glower could sometimes carry on for seemingly interminable weeks. This doesn't help to advance the public atmosphere that Chris and I were always aspiring to present to the customers. Believe me, an usherette who is sniffing and wiping her eyes as she tears a ticket can oddly disconcert customers out for an evening of pleasure together. Think of the last time you walked into a restaurant or stood in a supermarket checkout and were met with an unexpected frown or an ungracious gesture – it really brings a customer up short. Of course, all of this is true of any business which faces the public, but in the leisure industry good public manners and a unified staff are essential.

Oddly, one of the most unsettling culprits for wobbling this particular apple cart was the manager of us all, Chris. He, I gradually realised after four or five weeks of working with him, was in the throes of a complex relationship with the senior cashier. Mary, the cashier, was a good fifteen years older than him, a small wiry woman with dyed hair and a good laugh. Mary was Irish, hard-working, very loyal to Chris, and an experienced judge of the world and all its doings. As the effective team leader of the front-of-house staff she bent an unceasingly watchful eye upon whatever was happening, whether it was sudden crowds of schoolchildren all reaching for the chocolate bars, a doorman who had outstayed his cigarette break, or an unexpected visitor from head office. She was accurate and conscientious at all her tasks, at the paybox she was never flustered by false claims of underpayment of change into over-paying change for a banknote, or by routine rowdyism and muddle-making by other customers.

But she was, I believe, a bit muddled by Chris. He was her immediate boss and she enjoyed having his confidence: it is good always to have a sense that your superior trusts your judgement in professional matters. Their senses of humour meshed, too. A happy and effective and mutually useful relationship had been born. However, Chris wanted to advance to an intimate stage, and I think Mary wasn't keen. She was later to tell me, in a comfortable tone, that in the past they had been away on a holiday together, Chris having taken her with him to the Isle of Man for the annual speedway motorbike championships.

But now there was a tension, and it made Chris fume quietly. He would smoke and stare into space for twenty minutes at a time, then bang a ledger down onto his desk and start making entries furiously. He would work intently and growl if asked a question. It was wearing. A moody boss is a trial to any team: her or his emotional state will infect the working atmosphere for everyone. And when that atmosphere is effectively as unpredictable as the weather it can be very exhausting in the long-term.

I stumbled over so many minor administrative details in the next months that I believed Chris would soon be petitioning Mr Brown, the regional manager, to send him another assistant and take the present incumbent far away. Then one busy Friday evening, after all three of the last evening houses had finally gone in, Chris asked me to go for a drink across the road with him. We had been working alongside each other for about five months by now and this was the first time he'd ever made such an invitation. I was surprised. At the very least it was rather unorthodox for both managers to leave the premises during opening hours. However we would be away only half an hour at the most, and we would be quite literally just across the road. So over to The White Horse we stepped.

Being a Friday evening the din was terrific. The lights seemed harsh, and the smoke was very thick. All the tables and booths were crammed. At the back of the room people were standing four deep along the whole length of the bar, waiting to be served. Almost immediately I regretted not suggesting that we have this little outing on an afternoon or an early weekday evening. I couldn't see or hear as well as I wanted. And in about twenty minutes my lungs would begin to seize up.

Meaning to signal sociability and appreciation of Chris' unexpectedly friendly gesture, I pushed myself forward into the melee to get us both a drink. There were a lot of busy barman serving, so that it did not take as long as I had feared to get served. Weaving my return through the dense mob, I proudly carried the two pints of Guinness back across the packed room to the window ledge where Chris was waiting. I plopped the two pints on the ledge between us and lifted mine with a smile and a welcoming gesture. Chris gazed at me glumly. The corners of his moustache were curved severely downwards. 'Never touch the stuff,' he sneered wearily and turned away immediately and headed away into the throng to get his own drink. I had somehow formed the idea that Guinness was Chris' tipple of choice and had acted accordingly. I felt angry, ashamed of my stupidity, furious at his gracelessness, and sorry at the unnecessary expense. Guinness is comparatively expensive and I have never been that fond of stout for myself. In another five minutes Chris was back with a single pint of lager. He jerked his glass towards me with the briefest salutation and slurped the top two inches off at a gulp. I now had two pints of stout, neither of which I wanted. I forced myself to smile back and drank the first taste of my own glass.

'So – another busy night here as well, it seems…' I offered.

A long pause hung between us.

Chris gazed at me, then grunted non-committally into his dark full beard. He reached into his pocket, pulled out his cigarettes, stuck one into his face, and lit it. He exhaled slowly.

'Do you think we'll be full for the lates tonight?' I asked, trying again.

'Usually are.' Another pause. I tried once more.

'Marcela was late on shift again tonight.'

'She usually is.'

He stared into his pint. Now I was as cross as I was confused.

'So this is all very chummy,' I said, 'but did you have something you wanted to tell me, or to discuss, or a good joke to share?'

Now Chris did raise his eyes to mine.

'Nope. Just being sociable.' His eyes wandered away again.

I felt like a man in the sea who has been swimming too long. I stared out of the window, following his gaze. We could both see across the road, through the glass doors of the cinema, into the foyer. Mary and the other girls were refilling the chocolate counters and reloading the hot popcorn machine. A customer, having escaped briefly from Screen 2, this week showing an unfunny Peter Sellers comedy, was choosing a bag of sweets to console himself with through the second half. We watched this routine silently for a full minute or more. No one glanced back at us.

Slowly a shadow of understanding grew within me: Chris had probably complained of my shortcomings to Mary, but she, being naturally emollient, had suggested to him that young Nick meant well and wanted to be useful and if he, Chris, would just take a little trouble to get to know him, Chris would discover that young Nick might well evolve into a better resource than he at first appeared. Now I felt embarrassed and ashamed of myself and yet sorry for Chris too. There was something genuinely pitiable in the slump of his shoulders and the drop of his cigarette as he gazed across to the place where Mary was. The noise and the smoke of this full room were making me dizzy, as well as making me wheeze. I saw that Chris had only one swallow left in his glass. As he raised it to his mouth, I forced myself to slosh nearly half a pint of Guinness down my own neck in six long swallows. Putting the almost empty glass carefully down on the ledge next to the stupid full one that remained I said,

'Come on, back to work' and turned towards the door.

Chris followed immediately.

Through the months that followed Chris and I muddled along, even if we never became matey. Running the cinema kept us both busy enough. Indeed, keeping the whole operation moving forward was much like operating an elderly merchant ship. There was always a deal of bailing out to do, just to keep the thing afloat. You needed the crew to operate efficiently.

Najmah was one of the crew who did little bailing. She was a plump untidy young woman with a distracted air, her dark thick hair hanging like a limp curtain across her face. She had always to push it aside with a damp hand before she spoke. Najmah read fat heavy paperbacks on many topics, but nothing on time management or career advancement in the retailing environment that I could see. She had six afternoon / evening shifts every week, due on at 3.00pm each working afternoon. At about 3.20pm she would scurry past the glass of the main front doors every afternoon, glancing through to nod apologetically to whomever she could see. In another five minutes she would enter the foyer from the direction of the ladies loos, in her uniform, ready for work. 'Oh dear, where am I wanted?' she would gasp, shaking her head slightly at her own tardiness, but with a smile intended to be ingratiating, 'Oh dear, I'm so sorry…' I would tell her which hall she was needed in – or someone else would look at the roster – and off she would toddle to her post. This pattern was so regular, her contrition so apparent, her lateness so consistent that I guessed that perhaps there had to be some unavoidable other obligation; she was a caregiver in her family or she performed daily devotions just before work, perhaps. She was invariably late, always by the same twenty to twenty-five minutes. But lateness has an impact on other staff members, in as much as they are waiting to be relieved – and also they are held to account if they too are late with any regularity.

So I called Najmah in and asked her why.

'Oh, well,' she flustered, mumbling behind her hair, picking at the front of her blouse and looking down at the floor, 'I'm very busy, you know, and the bus is so slow, and I'm so sorry…' Her chin sank, her voice trailing off.

'Don't forget your lateness inconveniences other staff members,' I said. 'You always expect to get away at the end of your shift, don't you?' I asked her bowed head.

It was annoying really. She was disrupting the larger routine on a regular basis, and now she was behaving as though she'd been caught with the petty cash in her hand.

'Is there a specific reason for this persistent lateness?' I demanded firmly.

'Oh dear, oh dear, I will try harder, I'm sorry, I'm so sorry,' she whispered towards the floor, sniffing.

'Please do or I'll have to let you go,' I ended lamely.

But the lateness continued. I was annoyed, but a little intrigued too. In all other ways, Najmah was perfectly acceptable as a staff member. She did all her routine tasks properly, never smoked on duty or wandered away from her position or failed to check that the fire doors had been properly closed at the end of a show. She was a perfectly useful member of the team save for this chronic tardiness. After two more weeks of lateness I stopped her an hour's pay for each late day of that week. This brought her to the office to protest at the injustice of my behaviour. I suggested that there was no alternative save to let her go. Najmah agreed to try very hard to be better. But the results were the same. Then I finally had an idea. I appealed to Chris to modify her shift. She, unlike all the others, would start her afternoon shift an hour later, at 4.00pm. To my relief Chris agreed to this and so next payday I advised Najmah that from the following week she would now start an hour later. She straightened up and, pushing her lank dark hair out of her face, smiled a wide smile of profound gratitude at both of us. Now she'll be able to attend to her devotions without fretting I thought to myself. An elegant solution indeed.

And the next day Najmah came tottering down the slope towards the staff door at exactly 4.20pm. She smiled her routine apologetic smile at me as she passed the frontage. I actually glanced up to check the wall clock against my wristwatch. Yes, Najmah was still twenty minutes late. And there was to be no change, ever. Chris never dismissed her and Najmah continued to be twenty minutes late for five out of her six weekly shifts.

Yet it was Najmah who brought me the wallet full of money. Some months later, in the early autumn at about 10.45 one evening, at the very end of their shifts, she and Alan came to find me in the office, just as I was putting on my coat and switching off the office light. Alan was holding a substantial looking brown wallet.

'We found it in number 1 at the back, when we were checking round,' whispered Najmah, flicking her hair aside and looking up at me with her perennially worried smile.

Alan looked at me hard as he passed the find to me.

'Dude was loaded too, seems like.'

The correct form in this sort of situation is to open the purse or wallet or whatever in front of the staff member and establish whatever valuables may be to hand. Holding the fat wallet in before all three of us, I opened it up. There was a large lump of folded banknotes, a slim narrow stapled booklet of printed pages that I recognised as an old-style airline ticket, and a foreign identity card.

'Huh! Shee-it!' said Alan for all of us.

'Wow,' whispered Najmah.

I put the items on the office desk and very quickly assessed the cash.

'There looks to be more than £400 here,' I breathed. 'And an ID card too. Good work, guys. Someone is going to miss this lot soon, I'm sure. I'll put it in the safe right now and then I'll be sure to tell you what happens next.'

They departed, chattering between themselves. I turned off the office light and shut the door, put the alarm on, and stepped out into the corridor, locking the office door on all three locks. Down the stairs and across the silent empty foyer. Outside, through the glass doors, the street glowed softly under the streetlamps. I went down the back corridor buttoning my coat. I had my briefcase in my hand. That night I had achieved my hoped-for daily goal of managing to complete the final cashing up well before the end of the final film, so the day's takings had already been safely stowed in the local bank's night safe forty minutes or more earlier.

I tapped the code into the building's alarm box on the wall above the door, grasped the handle, opened the door and backed into the silent street. The pass door clicked shut. I gave the knob a routine twist. The door felt routinely solid. The night was clear and quiet, the traffic light but purposeful. I walked steadily up the hill towards the corner and the tube station, breathing the first freer breaths of being off duty. I was almost at the top of the slope when a man came sprinting round the corner.

He was breathing hard as he rushed past, his coat flapping, open. He careered down the hill away from me. I walked on some steps more. Then my tired brain engaged. Where would such a fellow be going? To what end? I turned and walked back to the corner and peered round. Squinting into the evening dusk I could see that he was already almost at the cinema frontage. In front of the glass doors the man stopped. He gazed into the dark foyer. Then he grasped a pair of door handles and shook them vigorously. I sighed and turned to walk back towards him. As I reluctantly approached, I could hear from nearly a hundred yards away, the sound of his knuckles rapping on the unavailing glass.

He was so intent on waking the dead that he did not see me approaching. The whole street seemed to be echoing with his pounding and rattling.

'Hey!' I called. He stopped banging. He looked round, his coat askew, his face strained.

Still holding the doors he gasped out,

'What chew wan'?'

He was so panicky I was a bit perturbed myself. I kept well back from him but asked,

'What's the matter – what are you trying to do?'

'I problem. I need boss of here. Is bad trouble.'

His accent was strong, from somewhere I couldn't place. Eastern Europe perhaps. I looked all around. If I had had the takings on me I would have been accompanied, but would he know that? I needed to be cautious.

'The cinema is closed,' I said to his back, not yet quite willing to reveal my hand.

He let go of the doors and turned. He looked anxious but not evasive or overconfident in his manner.

'I problem. I – I need – need hin-side,' he said with emphasis, having found the word. 'Inside – yes?' He stood stiffly, a stage pantomime of beseechment.

'Have you lost something?' I asked slowly.

He looked worried, blank. 'Plis?'

'You have lost something?' I repeated, on a rising inflection, then mimed looking at the ground for a dropped key or other small treasure.

'Ah yess – yes, good...' He beamed relief, his face registering the effect of a successful communication in a tense situation. 'My moan-ey, my moan-ey,' he urged, smiling tensely.

'Stay here,' I commanded in my best managerial tones, and pointed at the pavement in front of him. 'I am the manager of the cinema,' I went on in an almost biblical tone of self-declaration.

'Hah, wait, yess,' he nodded, frowning.

I walked past him a few yards more, back to the pass door. I turned away, trying to conceal the key process as much as possible. Inside I clicked the door shut and turned off the alarm. I stood very still and listened. If there was anything afoot, I would hear steps toward this door or a whistle to signal an accomplice. I had decided I would have time to turn the alarm back on again if they had anything with them less than a police battering ram, which seemed very unlikely. Nothing. I waited a full minute. Still nothing.

I turned and switched on the corridor light, climbed the steps to the office, unlocked the three locks, opened the door, turned on the light. I switched off the office alarm. My briefcase on the floor, I crossed the room to the safe then realised my keys were still in the briefcase. Back to the briefcase, open it, get the keys out, open the safe. The fat wallet was still there. All was calm. I took it up and dropped it on the desk while I locked the safe up again. I dropped the wallet into my overcoat pocket. Tapped the pocket. Alarm, office light, office door, three locks. The whole process in reverse.

Back down the steps. I listen again. Nothing. I turn on the building alarm, turn off the light, open the door and glance round. He hasn't moved a step but is watching me intently. I step out, turn my back to him, close the door, put the key away and turn to face him. A car or two swish by, softly. I walk up to him and put my bag down. I reach into my pocket and pull out the wallet. His eyes light up with immediate recognition as I hold it in front of me.

'I found this,' I say.

In one swift movement the man grabs the wallet out of my hand and thrusts it deep into his coat without so much as a further glance at it. Or me. He says not one word more. He immediately turns away, buttoning his coat tight and walks rapidly uphill away from me. I stand there alone watching his back grow smaller rapidly.

Another moment and he had vanished. Suddenly a great wave of exhaustion came over me. Turning, I picked up my bag, tightened my scarf and started back up the lamp-lit hill to recommence the long journey towards my bed.

The winter of 1981/82 had some hard weeks. The Classic Hampstead stood close to the southern margin of Hampstead Heath. At times it seemed like the cold air blew off the Heath straight into the foyer. The four pairs of glass double doors across the frontage seemed almost more an invitation to the cold than any sort of protection from it. The temperature dropped to an average of eleven degrees centigrade indoors. The water pipes were in danger of freezing, the chocolate bars on the sweetie counter were breaking the customers' teeth, the staff were dressed for survival. Over their uniforms they wore their own overcoats, scarves, hats, even mittens. Behind the sales counter Mary and her team stood wrapped and grim, looking like troops on the Russian front. There were two fan heaters in the foyer, high on the wall, above the doors. They whirred noisily but were utterly ineffective. The whole open foyer area was, at best, about four degrees warmer than the Shakespearian heath, bare and blasted, outside. All we lacked was a mad king, raving.

Chris had permitted Mary to pop a small electric heater on the floor inside her sales area. Entirely against Health and Safety regulations, of course, but the staff were all so ridiculously, bitterly cold, and they had to stand there, without any real shelter, a lot of the time. Mercifully the auditoriums were not so frigid. Each had double doors and a set of ceiling and wall heaters that did keep the sharp chill out of the air. Humans warm themselves too of course, especially when they are massed together. And in our office Chris and I enjoyed the perverse benefit of working in a windowless cubbyhole. We worked well wrapped up, true – but we were snug enough with a mug of tea each and the door shut.

One cold afternoon that week Mr Brown, the regional manager, turned up on one of his peripatetic visits. Trilby on head, coat collar turned up, he marched himself across the frozen foyer and surveyed the shivering clump of doormen and salesgirls swathed in frozen motley before him.

'Where are your uniforms?' he barked.

Mary gazed straight up into his pink face and said in her most sinister Irish tone,

'Here.'

She lifted her coat lapel and scarf aside for a brief second, allowing a momentary glimpse of the official brown and gold beneath, before immediately tucking herself up tightly again. Her smile would have cut a snake.

'Will you no take off yer hat, Sirr?'

Mr Brown glared and strode towards the stairs up to Chris' office.

Presently we could hear the echoes of a bellowing altercation from the office above. In a few moments Chris came down the stairs saying aloud that health and welfare regulations instructed that staff working areas be heated to a minimum of sixteen degrees centigrade and that until the company made adequate provision for this, he would allow his staff to dress as they were until the temperature lifted. Mr Brown was gesturing a show of remonstrance. Chris stood in his overcoat in the middle of the foyer and pointed with his mittened hand at one of the useless wall heaters.

'More noise than effect,' he said, looking at Mr Brown. 'Been on the repair list with head office since February last year. You've probably got my fourth request docket there in your briefcase.'

Mr Brown looked all round, pressed his lips together, and tucked his scarf down. He jerked his chin about half an inch towards Chris and turned towards the doors.

'Some salt for the steps would be good, too,' said Chris to his retreating back. 'Don't want the customers slipping on the ice that builds up. Council will only do the pavement...'

In a film we would all have applauded our noble leader. But at least we did all give him a real and grateful smile. And were even more impressed when later, during the first warm afternoon of April, a work team turned up to install four large ceiling heaters across the foyer. At least now we'd be better prepared when the next winter came.

Eventually air grew softer, the winds less bitter. There was light into the early evening, too. In a lunch hour it was possible to walk the 300 yards to the edge of the Heath proper and then sit on a park bench under the nearest trees, to look across the pond and commune with the swan family. Nine little grey cygnets, floating in a ragged little flotilla behind their parents. How many would last to the summer this year?

So it was finally spring at last, if not yet quite summer. And in spring, usually over the Easter bank-holiday weekend, the funfair comes to Hampstead. A travelling fair arrived at least once a year and would set up on the margin of the Heath just along from the cinema's corner and the adjoining cluster of shops. The fair's advent would signal quite a change in our sedate corner of north London. A week before the fair two large vans would appear during the night and start to mark out small plots on our local corner of the Heath. Over the next six days cables would be laid across the grass, a parking area marked out, larger waste bins would appear on would-be corners to what were, as yet, only a mirage of several thoroughfares of the fair yet to be. And early on Easter Friday morning two dozen very large trailers would have manifested themselves, along with an assortment of vans, domestic caravans, and motorhomes. They would be drawn up in an orderly phalanx behind the disorderly scaffolding that would soon become the rides. By lunchtime the lights would be on and the amplified music blowing a soft blurred ostinato into the breeze. As the afternoon wore on the customers would begin to appear, lank, expectant, prying, hungry. The sweet sharp smells of hotdogs and chips and vinegar and popcorn and candyfloss would rise into the wind and blow towards us all. By evening the whole area would be like a port when the fleet is in.

We could hear the delighted shrieks of fear from the whirligig rides, the raucous blare of the pop music played over the P.A., the crack of the rifles on the shooting range, the competing calls of the barkers on their competition stands, 'cahm on nah, dahn't be shy, everyone's a winnah'. Added to this was the shuffling roar of the crowd itself as it wandered, flirted, drank and gorged itself on fried treats. And then, finally, as evening's dusk came down over all, a little tired, a little muddy, a little drunk, some folk, casting about for further diversion, would notice the lights of the cinema twinkling their welcome just across the way.

The attention of everybody round about was also drawn to the cinema by the dwarf. The stout dwarf with an accordion. He was not, I think, strictly speaking, part of the fair's equipage, but he appeared annually on the same holiday weekend with his instrument strapped to his tum. He would parade along the top of the nine long shallow steps that led up to the cinema's frontage proper, playing a wheezy medley of tunes and grinning vaguely at everyone in sight. Sliding from *The Teddy-Bears' Picnic* into *Rock Around the Clock* then *My Way* then *Rule Britannia*, he would play sometimes only eight or ten bars of each before segueing with a wobble into the next part of his narrow repertoire. The effect of the musical wobble was amplified by the shake he would give to his impressive belly in order to draw attention to the small metal cup attached by wire to the front of his instrument.

The cinema steps, of course, were private property, and so it fell to me to approach this musical maestro and tell him repeatedly to retreat. He would glance up at me, sneer mildly, and then withdraw to the pavement below, where his shallow serenade would continue unabated. If there was a queue of customers waiting for a popular film to start, my hourly remonstrance would immediately become part of his act.

'Can you please keep off the steps?' I would urge. Mr Accordion would cock his head on one side, jerk his chin towards me but keep his eyes fixed on his audience:

'Not a music lover, then, hey?'

Eventually I thought of a response:

'On the contrary,' I shouted ringingly, 'it's because I'm a devoted lover of music that I need you off these steps.'

But Mr Accordion's timing was better than mine, and he would get the laugh, not I.

The crowd that came in on those Easter weekends was always tempered by the spirit of the fair. They were livelier, more dishevelled, and wore t-shirts that were now creased and lipstick that was now smeared. The odours of the fair came with them as did the same spirit of easy come, easy go, of distraction for its own sake. If we had a Clint Eastward cop drama or a Bill Murray comedy we would often sell out earlier than usual. The boys would be more inclined to pull away from romances even if the girls expressed a preference to see one. A date at the fair is not one where you are striving to make a good first impression. Probably more friendships ended than began in the cinema's dark over those long, noisy, tiring weekends.

One day, only a few weeks after the fair had reversed its magic and dematerialised itself, Chris had a surprise for me. Mr Brown had been in on one of his routine visits that morning, and I had been glad to find duties for myself elsewhere in the building. As I crossed the foyer carrying a large bundle of fresh rolls of toilet paper to the downstairs gents (oh, the glories of working in show business) Mary called out to me.

'Chris wants you in the office.' Having refreshed the bathroom stationery I mounted the stairs to the office.

Chris glanced across the littered desk at me.

'Mr Brown was here.' 'Yes, I saw.' 'How'd you like to be an assistant in the West End?'

'Chris, that's a promotion, no? I wasn't expecting that.'

His beard and moustache were so thick I couldn't be sure of his expression, but his eyes were cheery.

'No. I'll bet you didn't. But he does. He's got a couple of gaps because of other people's promotions, and he wonders if you'd suit down at Charing Cross Road. That's where they have the all-nighters.' This was a lot to take in.

I asked, 'So what happens here?'

Now he was smiling.

'Same old bollocks, I shouldn't wonder. Brown'll send us someone, don't you worry. He needs an answer.'

I replied to Chris that I'd tell him tomorrow or the day after at the latest.

All through the evening and the next morning I meditated intensely upon this offer. Chris was being civil, but I suspected he wanted me gone if he had a choice. I was much happier than I had been at Oxford, but that was because the Classic Hampstead was essentially a successful business, I was not hand-cuffed to a human catastrophe waiting to happen, as I had been in Oxford. Moving to a central London hall would be a career advance, even though there'd be a whole new set of routines to master. Also Martha's flat at Latimer Road would be no less handy for the

West End than it was for Hampstead. I decided I'd better seize the chance offered, but I'd ask for a raise so that I appeared not too desperate.

To my surprise when I phoned Mr Brown the following morning, he offered a raise anyway.

'Hundred and ten a week with the central London weighting,' he declared. 'You can start Monday fortnight. That's the third of next month. Good luck.'

Click. The line went dead.

Chris was quite unperturbed when I told him I'd be leaving Hampstead in fifteen days. As that final fortnight wore on I became increasingly excited about the whole idea of a new posting. I thought to ring the manager at Charing Cross Road to suggest that I might come and visit him informally when I was next in the centre of town. And I would have to advise Martha that my hours and daily routine might change, but that was unlikely to present a problem.

But my adventures at Hampstead were not yet over. On the Thursday evening that week we were surprisingly busy. We had two near sell-out houses and were half-full in the third. Mary and her team had sold a lot of chocolate and ice-cream and plastic cups of powdered coffee. Trevor and Rex had been professionally busy making sure the naughty boys in the queues all paid before they entered and behaved thereafter. I'd been busy all evening on redeployment of staff and re-supply to sales, as need arose. At 8.45pm the main films had all been on screen the regulation ten minutes so the foyer staff had cleared up and set off home. Trevor and Rex were keeping their four relaxed but watchful eyes on the mostly docile customers. I was busy counting banknotes into neat piles of a hundred. Credit card payments for cinema tickets were still rare at this time: not unknown by any means but, as yet, not routine with us.

So squat bundles of banded banknotes, as preferred by bank robbers and drug dealers, were a common occurrence. I sorted the cash, checked it against what I expected to have, completed the banking docket and stuffed this final roll of money into a bank wallet. The petty cash and books were locked in the safe along with the prepared wallet of the evening takings. I pushed the office door shut so it was locked and went to see the houses come out.

At about 10.40pm the films began to roll their credits. In another ten minutes the halls were all dark, and the projectionists had locked the projection suites and gone home. Trevor and Rex had declared all clear and chained the emergency exits and the front doors. I asked Rex to stay on for the routine five minute walk of 150 yards to the bank's night safe with me. This was usual when there was cash to deposit.

'Ah checks yah inna club later, mon,' said Trevor to Rex as he turned to go.

I went upstairs, opened the safe, transferred the black leather bank wallet into my briefcase, locked the safe up tight, bundled into my coat, switched on the office alarm, switched off the office light, turned the key in all three of the office locks, descended the stairs. I met Rex in the passage.

'Time to go – you ready?'

He nodded with a friendly grunt. Down the passage we went. I set the building alarm, turned off the light, followed Rex out of the small pass door. It was a dry fine night, not too cold. We walked up the slope together towards the bank.

Rex turned to me and asked almost shyly,

'So is it true youse be gawn nex' week?' His tone seemed quite regretful. I was touched.

'Yep – I'm moving to the West End. It'll be a big new thing for me…' A shadow fell over us. A sudden voice growled very close, 'Shut up you fucking nigger' and punched Rex savagely.

Rex was caught completely off guard and fell to the ground hard. Immediately the man kicked him as he lay there. Rex gave a soft groan. I was utterly bewildered. Why this racist attack and why now? Then I felt a sharp tug on my right arm and a punch to my right side. Sudden pain. I looked round to my right but already the two figures were fleeing, one of them carrying my briefcase away at speed. I was in pain but Rex was groaning and his face was very bloody. He was holding his side. I made no attempt to run after the robbers, I couldn't have caught them anyway.

'Can you get up? We're just by the hospital,' I wheezed down at him.

I leaned over Rex. He was gasping, utterly winded.

'Can you move?' I asked him, feeling frightened and rather uncertain. I didn't want to move him, and I wasn't sure that I could lift him even if I had wanted to. Rex groaned again.

'Where de fucker gawn, mon?'

'Take it easy Rex. There were two of them. I've been robbed of the cinema takings. They're long gone. We're just by the hospital here. Let's go in and get checked out.'

'Nah,' said Rex as he sat up slowly. 'Gonna find 'em fuckers and do 'em up good.'

He leant on his arm and looked around past me. I offered a hand to him. He took it and pulled himself up, and I felt such a sudden rush of pain that I nearly fell down on top of him myself. He grabbed me and pulled me back upright, and we stood leaning together like exhausted partners in a dance.

'Ah, mon – we'd better get in ta dem doctors, I'm t'inking.'

Not quite arm in arm we shuffled the few steps into the hospital A&E department.

Inside there were bright lights and the usual seated rows of weeping children with anxious parents and bleeding drunks and confused old folk. Rex and I were such an odd pair we attracted the attentions of a young houseman very quickly.

'We've just now been attacked in the street outside,' I gasped out at him. 'Mugged really. My friend here's been badly punched. Can you help us, please?'

The houseman led us to a pair of curtained cubicles. He summoned a nurse and then took Rex into the next door cubicle.

Giving me a very considering look the nurse asked me,

'Are you hurt?'

I said I had a pain in my side but my friend had been punched and kicked and was far worse off.

'The doctor is looking after him. Let's look at you,' she said briskly.

I sat down on the examination couch, and just as I did so I noticed a small diamond shaped tear in the right side of my leather coat. She had evidently seen this from the outset. She helped me unzip the coat and very gently pulled it open. There was a small patch of blood on the right side of my sweater, over the lower ribs.

'Can you get that off?' she asked. I lifted the sweater and the bloom of blood was now on my shirt, but no larger than before. The nurse helped me off with my shirt and we both looked. There was a large red bruise lightly seeping blood.

'Have you been in a fight?' she asked.

'No, I was robbed – I think he must have punched me.'

'He hit you with something sharp I would guess. But you were very lucky – your leather coat protected you from much of it.'

She bathed the wound and dressed it. Now that knew I was wounded my side began to throb abominably. When I came out of the cubicle area there was Rex, his face and right ear very bandaged. He looked grey and weary.

'How are you?' I whispered.

'Me side hurts bad. Waitin' for de x-ray result. Ah wants t'git home to me yard bot nahbody listen at me.'

We both sat on a bench. In a while the houseman returned and told Rex he hadn't broken anything but they wanted to keep him in overnight, for observation.

'Nah. Me gwan home, mon. Me woman she's a nurse too, y'know. Jes' like you got in dis place, mon. For real. She know awl de right ting t'do, y'know.'

He looked at both of us, trying to be reassuring. After a little more insistence from Rex the young man agreed that he could call his nurse friend and that Rex could go home but only if he promised to return immediately if he felt unwell. I agreed to stay on and give the routine report to the police. Then I too would be allowed to go home with a fistful of painkillers. As I sat there I began to collect my thoughts. I needed to find a phone to report the robbery to Chris and to Mr Brown. My briefcase had gone off with the thieves. That meant they had my set of keys to Martha's flat and my cheque book and cheque card, not to mention my paperback of *Fear and Loathing in Las Vegas*, my favourite pocket torch, and my Ventolin inhaler. A short time later a young policeman turned up and wrote down a very brief statement and my contact details. I agreed to give a more detailed account as soon as I was asked.

On the phone both Mr Brown and Chris remained professional even though I had to advise them that the company was poorer by slightly more than £1,200. I then had to ring Martha to tell her what happened in the briefest terms and ask her to let me in when I arrived back on the doorstep. As luck would have it, my wallet was still in my back trouser pocket. It was now nearly midnight so, feeling rather shaken still, I decided to ring for a cab to get home. In thirty minutes more I was ringing the door bell in Latimer Road.

It was a great relief to get indoors and home at last. The sense of shock, of a near run thing, of the 'what-if...' of the whole event was beginning to dawn on me. Martha and Ray were civil, even sympathetic, but I felt rather drawn. A shared cup of hot chocolate and twenty minutes of quiet conversation and it was now past 2.00am. I took two more painkillers and then we fell into our several beds. A sadder and a wiser man I rose the morrow morn.

And my ribs throbbed rather. I took the day off and rested in bed but I accepted an invitation to go into the cinema the next day to give a full report on the robbery to the police and later that same day to the company's insurance investigator along with Mr Brown and Chris. Later that week Chris interviewed Rex, but after that I heard no more. And at the end of the week it was time for me to move on to the Charing Cross Road cinema.

The Classic Cinema, 35 Charing Cross Road, 1977

Designed by William Hancock, the Cinema de Paris opened in 1910 with its entrance on Bear Street. In 1926 it was reconstructed and re-opened as the Cameo with 476 seats. It was a newsreel cinema from 1932 to 1956, known as the Cameo Revudenews from 1936. The name changed to Cameo Royal with the screening of foreign language X Certificate films. The Classic Cinemas chain took it over in 1967. Once the Cannon Group acquired it, the cinema was renamed the Cannon Royal in 1985. The hall closed in 1988 and was demolished the following year. The retail and office accommodation built on the site is known as Cameo House.

City of London: London Metropolitan Archives
http://collage.cityoflondon.gov.uk 12877

The Classic Cinema, Leicester Square Spring 1982

The Classic, Leicester Square, was a fraud. It wasn't in Leicester Square at all. Its very narrow frontage faced onto Charing Cross Road, just along from the Garrick Theatre and opposite Cecil Court, that lovely alley of bookshops. Indeed, in those days most of Charing Cross Road was lined with independent and second-hand book shops, and the street was the effective border that lay between the different but complementary attractions of Soho and Covent Garden. Like all border areas Charing Cross Road had a raffish, untidy charm that was highly permeable: the food and permissiveness on the one side passed easily over to the culture and sophistication of the other, and vice versa.

This cinema was a real oddity. A gnarled survivor from the days of the newsreel cinema era, it was now a sort of lowbrow first-run house by day and a flea-pit of last resort by night. After paying for admission under the glass of a narrow paybox window perched out on the street the punter turned to walk along a very cramped corridor lined in dark wood, stained to suggest mahogany, and passed through a narrow curtained doorway directly into the auditorium. She or he immediately found themselves four feet from the bottom of the screen, half blinded by the projected image towering above and half deafened by the nearside speaker that boomed towards them. The customer now had to turn hard left and walk up the slope towards the back, looking along the rows to find a seat. It was a patently ridiculous arrangement and had the odd side-effect of making it impossible to enter the cinema without being visible to everyone else in the hall if they chose to notice the twitch of the curtain which hung effectively right on the edge of every single viewer's eye line.

The films here were the bottom end of the first-run release circuit: foreign language trash, the promise of whose salacious content was both guaranteed and protected by the convenience of sub-titles. *The Love Lives of the French Chambermaids* would be a representative title. On the posters outside cartoon demoiselles clad only in black underwear and improbable heels would be folding sheets on ornate beds above a caption that read, 'The naked truth about the city of sin'. Not porn really, merely smut undressed as exotica.

The all-night programmes were peculiar also, but in a very different way. The Charing Cross cinema had evolved a programming style that was, in my experience, quite unique in the whole of London. Back then the West End was effectively the only district that stayed open all night. The pubs proper had to shut at 11.00pm but the whole area was rife with hotels and nightclubs, members-only drinking clubs, casinos, clip joints and late opening restaurants of every degree of legality. A Soho building might commonly have a strip joint in the basement, a very smart foreign restaurant at street level, a 'private' drinking club on the first floor, and a couple of whores operating from the top floor flat reached by steep stairs from a small side doorway in the street. The neighbouring building might typically be a bespoke tailor's shop front with a film production office above and a violin-maker on the top floor. In such an environment a cinema that served its clientele until 9.00am every morning seems merely compassionate.

At 10.45pm or so the French chambermaids would have passed through the projector for the last time that day. The customers, surely much wiser than when they came in, would totter out to the street for a late bus home. Inside there would be a rapid tidy round, and the last tardy somnambulates would be hustled out of the doors. At 11.00pm we would now sell tickets to an all-night programme of westerns or spy stories or war dramas or something similar. Four or five features that were timed, with intervals, to run through until breakfast. A breakfast which we also sold. The ticketing scheme for this was a brilliant wheeze. The films were old material that had really no commercial life in them. (Remember that the video re-release of back catalogue films was only beginning at this time.) The cinema rented a quintet of worn-out prints for a flat fee of about £75 a title. But by offering each customer a small cellophane packet of biscuits and a paper cup of instant coffee each (the advertised 'free breakfast') at the time of the ticket sale, the house was able to charge about £9 a seat. (This was close to double what a normal admission would be for a single new release title in the area.) This breakfast was never declared to the film rental company, and so the all-nighters were decently profitable even with the overtime costs. The paper cups could also be refilled and the biscuits renewed throughout the night, though now at a far from moderate additional fee to the captive audience within.

The company was effectively running the cheapest hotel in the West End, and indeed a few regular customers used the cinema in just this sense. It was also a refuge for those who had missed the last tube home and did not fancy a long night bus journey. Streetwalkers sought occasionally to bring a client in to make use of the convenient dark, but this was always seriously resisted by the night manager. He would be liable if there was ever any sense that the cinema was facilitating a criminal trade. Of course assignations of a less obviously commercial nature were harder to moderate. People might fall in love with total strangers once they were actually in the hall, mightn't they? So long as they were quiet and kept most of their clothes on, we tried not to see more than was unavoidable. But in fact such behaviour was comparatively rare. Mostly we sold those worn old seats to single men, men who dozed fitfully through the night. A customer was more likely to be kept awake by snores from the seats around him than by the sounds of rending cloth and passionate gasps. After the first hour or so those grey men lay slumped in their coats, while the films, unregarded, flickered in the half-light above them. Apart from the light traffic to and from the toilets and to and from the coffee and biscuit stand, they remained quietly immobile throughout the night. As dawn freshened, and the final set of credits fluttered up the screen, the projectionist would throw on all the lights and turn the sound up loudly. Then in the ringing silence that followed they would stiffly gather their wraps and file out of the door. If you have ever endured a long night flight in a full economy-class airline cabin you will know how those rumpled punters felt as they stepped into the pale light of a Soho early morning.

The manager of the more conventional day programme was John Pond. John was lithe, strong, neat, and very observant. He had a brisk manner and didn't smoke or drink. He was from St Lucia and certainly didn't plan on spending the remainder of his life in London. His account pages were neat, his company documents shelved in a tidy row, his staff well trained. In an area of London that tended towards incoherence and extravagant behaviour, he was pleasant and modest at all times. In fact, John was the only manager I ever knew who didn't, in one way or another, routinely convey a sense of strain. His calm impression of confidence made a refreshing contrast to the rather lurid environment of the entertainment factory that was the West End. It was delightful to be welcomed by such a man and to be trained towards his habits of work.

John proved to be a good mentor. He was meticulous but not obsessive, serious but not dull. He kept the small office very neat and always made two cups of tea any time he was brewing. As we were a West End house, we were required by the firm to wear a dinner jacket after 6.00pm every evening. John's dinner suit was always well-brushed and his shoes were always gleaming. His secret joy was tennis. He loved the game and played it regularly on his days off. In my experience most cinema managers took no more exercise in their leisure hours than searching for the TV remote, but John was an impressive exception. And he had refined his dedication to the sport by annually pre-booking his two weeks holiday entitlement every year to coincide exactly with Wimbledon fortnight. He would attend in person any matches he could in the first week and then watch all the later sold-out games on the screen at home. The only time John ever looked at me with something suggesting respect and admiration was when I told him that my granny lived in Wimbledon and that if the wind was blowing in the right direction you could hear the crowd at the matches – and the umpire calling the points – even before the signal arrived on her TV screen.

He had a small staff that had been with him for years and were very loyal. Sam was the front-of-house doorman for most of the day and was supported by Jake in the evenings. Sam was careful and deliberate and easily confused by changes in routine. But within his routine he was highly functional and seemed unperturbed by any rudeness he met from customers who mistook his deliberateness for stupidity. He lived in a hostel and his clothes were often a little stained and grubby. But he was willing and always wanting to be useful if he could. Sam's co-worker Jake was a retired soldier. He would tell much-repeated tales of service duty in Aden and Cyprus and Egypt on any occasion. He brooked no nonsense from rowdies – Jake had also had a season as a prison warder – so he was quite fearless in dealing with any kind of belligerence. He could be very useful in a predicament. And I was soon to need him.

I'd only been on solo duty as manager about half a dozen times at Charing Cross before we had a crisis: the crisis of the punter who couldn't leave. The last evening performance of *Swedish Massage Girls in Bangkok* had just ended. We now had fifteen minutes to clear the house, balance the takings, rinse down the toilets and do the hand-over to the night manageress and her team. At this crowded moment at the end of our working day Sam came and knocked on the door to tell me someone was refusing to leave.

'He's asleep, Mr Scudamore. But he won't go.'

Sam spoke in his usual breathy monotone but was watching my face carefully to see what to do next. This sounded a bit odd, so I followed him up the narrow passage into the hall. There was indeed just one single customer halfway up the aisle slumped in a chair, one seat in from the end of the row. I walked up and bent down. No smell of alcohol.

'Hello, Sir,' I said loudly. 'Time to go. The programme's over.'

No response whatever. I looked at him more closely. Collar and tie, ordinary mackintosh. But his head was at an odd angle. I reached out, grasped his shoulder and gave him a deliberate shake.

'Hello Sir!' I bellowed.

He fell forward and hit his chin on the seat in front. He flopped over the chair, inert. Like a punch in the chest I realised he was clearly dead. I turned to Sam.

'Sam, put the cleaner's lights on and then go find Jake. Tell the paybox not to sell tickets. Understand? No tickets. Get Jake. Wait at the front. Okay?'

He nodded, looking very unhappy, but went trotting off. He flicked on the cleaner's lights as he left the hall.

Under the harsh glare of the 200-watt cleaner's lights the hall now looked as grubby as it possibly could. Worn carpet runner, battered seats, filthy curtains over the screen, cigarette butts all over the floor. And this poor gentleman, quite still. He was clean-shaven and was wearing an old Burberry raincoat and old brogues. I was disinclined to touch him, yet he had to be moved. Jake came bustling up behind me.

'Sam says yer wants me, Sir... Oh lor. He's a gonner for sure. Poor ol' bugger. Blimey. Ave yer rung the police?'

I felt sick and turned away. I said,

'Just found him. I think you'd better stay here for a moment. I'll go to the office and make the call.'

Instead I went to the front and found Charlie, one of the night team, already taking over in the paybox. Sam was there, gazing into the street. He was looking very puzzled. The night show regulars were already forming into a queue, shifting uncomfortably from foot to foot on the pavement outside.

'Sorry gents, there will be quite some delay tonight,' I shouted to the faces at the front.

'Charlie, I'm going to turn off the front lights, there won't be a show for at least an hour. Don't sell any tickets. Tell them to go home. Tell them there's a problem with the electricity current.'

Charlie looked unconvinced but nodded.

I reached up behind him and pulled down the lever on the switch box. Immediately the greater part of the whole cinema canopy and signage lights blinked into darkness. Charlie was lit only by the sepulchral glow of his desk light. The crowd beyond now groaned collectively and began to expostulate amongst themselves and then with Charlie. I fled back down the corridor to the office and rang 999 and asked for both an ambulance and the police. In less than five minutes a police car was at the front. Three policemen in yellow vests came up the corridor, their walkie-talkies squawking static loudly. I led them up the corridor into the bare and silent hall. Jake was still where I had left him. He looked relieved at the presence of authority. I sent him off to support Charlie at the front.

'I found him slumped at the end of the show, about ten minutes ago,' I said.

The three policemen gazed at the poor fellow. They asked me if I'd moved him so I admitted to having shaken him in an attempt to wake him. They asked if he was a regular, did I know anything about him, had he been behaving strangely when he came in, all the obvious questions. They examined the floor for clues all around the body. One of them produced a camera and took pictures. The ambulance team arrived next, but by then the police had taken charge and decided to send for a crime scene team, so the ambulance was sent away empty. I felt very sad and seriously out of my depth. In five minutes more I left them to it.

It was clear that there couldn't be a show that night and so I went to find Mary the night manager. She was from Thailand, very petite and trim. Mary tended towards fitted jackets and narrow skirts with good nails and hair. She was also very hard-working and ambitious. She worked a full ten-hour day job at a local hotel – she was head of housekeeping and managed all the chambermaids – and then came on to the cinema to do the night shifts for six nights a week.

Mary hadn't been deceived by the power-cut cover story for a moment.

'Hi Nick, you look bad. What is the matter? It is not the electric, is it?' She flashed her brown eyes searchingly at me.

'No – there was a dead body at the end of the last house. Sam found him. I've called the police. I think he may have just died in his seat. It's horrible to think about. Poor chap. He looks so ordinary.'

'Not a druggie, then?'

'I don't know. He has good shoes and his clothes were clean enough.'

'We get all sorts in this place. Don't worry. Not your fault. You want some tea? Then I'll call Mr Brown.' 'Thanks. I'll do it. He will want to ask questions. Then I'll call John.'

I rang Mr Brown at home. He was so taken aback that he was almost civil. I explained that the police were on site already and that Mary would take over but that there didn't look to be any chance of running any of the routine programme that night.

'Quite right. They can all sod off to the night buses,' he growled. 'Do 'em good. Mothball the place, send the staff home, make sure everything is secure and we'll meet in the morning. Put Mary on. Night.'

Mary spoke to him briefly, standing up beside the phone as if Mr Brown was there in person. She hung up. She stood stiffly, her face thoughtful. I said,

'Let's go put the shutters up. Ring Jeff in the box and tell him to unspool and shut down. Then we'll have that tea.'

At the front the queue had dwindled down to four or five shuffling uncertain shapes. I told Charlie to lock up and close the paybox.

'You and Sam go home. There'll be no show tonight.'

'What about tomorrow?' asked Charlie.

'Give us a ring before you come in. But they won't want to lose two nights' business, will they?'

'Nah. You're right there. Well, night then, Mr Scudamore.'

Mary and Sam and I pulled the front shutter almost to the ground. Then I retreated to the hall. The police were finishing up. They confirmed that the ambulance team had suggested that the poor man had passed away from a sudden stroke, but that there would need to be an autopsy. Two of them were leaving, but one would remain until the body was collected which would be within the next hour or so.

'Did you find any ID?' I asked.

'Yes. He has a wallet and a diary. Picture of the wife and kiddies, too. Lives in Eltham apparently. We'll ring the local station. Someone will go and visit the wife. We can take it from here. You will be summoned to give evidence to the coroner, possibly. And a detective will visit you tomorrow or the next day. Will you be here tomorrow, Sir? And I'll need to take your address.'

'Oh yes. Certainly. And I'm going to make a spot of tea. Any takers?' I was trying to match his matter-of-fact tone. They declined politely.

Back in the office Mary was being reassuring. 'S'all right, now. You did a good job, Nick. It's nasty, a thing like that. Have the tea. A nice biscuit for you?'

I felt a really strong urge to just run away. But I needed to be calm and orderly and not leave anything undone that needed doing.

'There's one policeman left,' I said. 'They're just waiting for the body to be collected. Then we can go home, I suppose.'

We drank the tea together, in thoughtful silence.

In a short while there was a bang on the shutter at the front. Mary leapt up immediately and skipped to the front, her heels clicking as she went. I hid in the office while the poor fellow was transported away. I felt thoroughly sick at heart. But in ten minutes more we were slipping into our coats and stepping out through the side door.

Back at Latimer Road all was still. I didn't feel like waking Martha and Ray. In the kitchen I turned on only the side lights. I made a fresh pot of good quality loose tea very slowly and quietly, paying close attention to all the details I usually skipped, like warming the pot and stirring the brew and letting it steep properly. I chose the prettiest cup and saucer I could see, then opened a fresh bottle of milk. I sat down and poured the tea through the strainer, inhaling the smell of the Assam deeply. The pale, yellow colour was lovely. I sat still and drank it down in slow grateful sips. When the second cup was empty it was time for bed.

The Moulin Five Screens, Windmill Street, 1977

Opened in 1910, in the early 1930s this cinema became the Piccadilly News Theatre. After the Second World War it was renamed the Cameo Cinema with the name Moulin, inspired by the famous Moulin Theatre across the street, added in 1961. The Classic chain, later part of Cannon Cinemas, took over in 1972. It closed suddenly on 10th April 1990 and was later converted into a restaurant.

Cinema Theatre Association Archive

The Moulin Cinema, Windmill Street Summer 1982

A further way of picking up experience and training and also of signalling to the company that you were seeking advancement was to take on cover duties at other houses whenever they were offered to you. As there were five cinemas in close proximity to Piccadilly Circus these temporary changes of posting were easily managed.

It was a way of establishing professional credibility with colleagues who might, in the future, solicit for your services on a more permanent basis when the need eventually arose. And cover work was paid at overtime rates if you did the shifts on your leisure days.

And thus I entered the twilight world of soft-core porn cinemas, never an elevating experience, though it does improve your ability to judge character. The world of porn cinemas has effectively vanished from the West End nowadays, for two reasons: the easing of censorship and the internet. But in the first half of the 1980s VHS video were not yet fully established in the home market and so the soft porn cinemas still had a traditional place at the very bottom of the economic food chain of cinema exhibition. The two halls I was to grow most familiar with had been news cinemas in their earlier lives.

Before television all cinemas had screened news items. A fifteen-minute programme of short actualities, usually of predictable events like national sporting fixtures or film and theatre premieres, or the Queen's birthday celebrations, or arrivals of glamorous and exciting foreign folk at our airports, as well as occasional footage of some natural disaster in a faraway place were commonly included in a routine cinema programme. These items were all linked by a stentorian voice-over narration delivered in a relentlessly upbeat tone. News cinemas were a development of this idea: by running a thirty-minute version of the same type of news and variety programme and adding to it one or two cartoon shorts and a short bland travelogue of some lush part of the former Empire, as well as a little local advertising, these cinemas were able to run programmes of about sixty minutes total duration. Admission was cheaper than a first-run house and they were often sited near transport hubs like bus terminals or railway stations or close to popular shopping areas.

The programmes were continuous, that is they ran on a sixty-minute loop and people would enter and sit for as long as they liked. In areas where people had time to kill such houses could do a very steady trade. News cinemas required a lot of policing inasmuch as they were a magnet for socially marginal behaviour all the way from sleeping off a long night's drinking to random private assignations of a more impromptu nature... Historically these small news houses steadily lost their audience as television established itself within the larger culture. Their owners found two alternative uses for them – cartoons or porn.

At Victoria and Baker Street stations were two of my favourites. As a child, when looking for a treat, I would petition my parents to be 'taken to the cartoons'. Perhaps today's nine-year-olds solicit a meal at a favourite hamburger chain restaurant with the same avid anticipation of easy gratification as I did at those dingy cinemas. An anticipation which my kind parents would occasionally fulfil but with the same slight sense of failure and regret as modern parents must feel in a convenient burger chain. This is a treat which the dear child will soon have to be discouraged from selecting. But not today.

The other use was porn. In the liminal spaces of the West End, those redundant former news cinemas became places where soft-core sex was screened for around thirteen hours a day. 'Uncensored sex films' the Moulin cinema hoardings screamed. The films were sold with the most lurid advertising legally permitted, both trailers and poster-work hinting at scenes of behaviour that would have shamed ancient Babylon. But the reality was flaccidly different. The films were usually atrociously dubbed and trimmed foreign titles that were double- or triple-billed together into programmes of around three hours and then run as a continuous show throughout the day, from 11.00am to midnight, seven days a week.

The films featured lots of heavy breathing and serial disrobing but no actual sex. Those carnal displays had been literally scissored out of the print by the distributor before it was rented to the cinema. Thus, while the film had not been formally submitted to the British Board of Film Classification (BBFC) and so did not bear an official 'X' certificate (and thus could be promoted as 'uncensored'), it had in fact been bowdlerised to the extent that it now fell just inside the lines of current permissibility. The sexual congress promised was always consensual, adult, and heterosexual. And missing. A dressing gown would fall to the floor. A lascivious glance would be exchanged between the two lustful combatants. The assets of the actress, above the waist and from the rear, would be displayed in all their glory. The combatants would advance and grasp. Then cut. With an audible click on the soundtrack the hero was back in the street, decently re-trousered and walking away from the site of his tryst. Not even the tidiness of a fade to black. Just a shudder and then a jerk into the next scene. This bizarre 'cinema interruptus' might occur six or eight times in the course of a narrative that would become increasingly fragmented as it advanced towards its anti-climax.

The Moulin Cinema complex lay on the very edge of Soho – just above Piccadilly Circus. It was the cinema equivalent of the chain steak restaurants that line Shaftesbury Avenue, the ones that have huge windows through which red velvet banquettes are clearly visible. These places offer very average steaks at rather high prices served by underpaid staff. They look like glamorous and expensive restaurants to foreigners who don't know where else to go, and the management never anticipates repeat business. The Moulin was a similar false portal to the reputed pleasures of Soho: garishly inviting, promising much, delivering little.

The Moulin Cinema complex occupied the street level and basement of an otherwise utterly nondescript office block. The Moulin's foyer had a low ceiling lined with grubby Styrofoam tiles with neon strip-lights hanging from them. Behind this uninspiring foyer there were five screens, each seating about one hundred. The customers were always men, almost always alone, though very occasionally there might be a feisty trio of lads. Most days the shows ran utterly without incident. The customers sat slumped and still, alone in the gloom, an empty seat between each, gazing with a sort of unfocused pale hope up at the grey and flickering screens. There was no misbehaviour, even of a solitary nature. The halls smelled of sweat and cigarettes. The only recurrent problem was punters wandering from one auditorium into the next. I could never decide if such a one was genuinely trying to cheat the company out of a second admission charge or had simply gone to the lavatory mid-film and then just turned the wrong way coming out and drifted into the nearest hall – and not noticed any change in protagonists or narrative.

The Moulin was managed by Miss Kaitlin, a Scotswoman of middle years from the Orkneys. She lived on instant coffee, cigarettes, and Celtic fantasy novels of the sword-and-sandal variety. She was short, efficient and justly unimpressed by me. However, she was fair. After my having covered a couple of leave days for her she consented to my doing more of them from time to time; this meant that I could easily work one of my rest days and so pick up a little very useful overtime pay. As the cinema had a continuous admissions policy, there was little variation in the day's business cycle, the shows just tending to be fuller in the later evening screenings. The staff were all worker-bees perfectly adapted to their specific roles. I don't think Miss Kaitlin either lost or took on a single new face the whole year or so that I worked alongside her.

The chief doorman was David, a sallow youth with a shaved head who spoke broad cockney and frequented gyms on his days off. He never lost his Tippex tan. David would flash each punter a mildly conspiratorial half-smile as he steered them towards the paybox should they show any hesitancy about crossing our grotty threshold into the Moulin's palace of fleshly delights.

Gavin was the cashier at the Moulin. He was young, trim, and quiet. He was also punctual and accurate. He worked a lot of overtime, and sat reading in the paybox for hours, but so discreetly that for weeks I didn't even realise that he was breaking regulations. But his habits of discretion did not inhibit his forming calm friendships with many of the staff. He was one of those quiet people who seem to inspire confidences from others. I learned later that he was an orphan and had been brought up in care homes. Perhaps this explained his well-developed powers of empathy.

There was also the very elderly Irene, already well into her pensionable years, who walked in from Islington to the cinema every day. And then walked home again at the end of every shift. She was wraith-thin, wore heavy make-up under a wig of incandescent yellow so patently false that it bore its own kind of truth. Irene was almost bent double with age yet carried a small tray of ice-creams continuously between all the halls for hours at a time. She sold but few and yet was an excellent company look-out. 'No film in number three,' she might tell me after tapping on the office door, and I would nip along to number three to find the dozen residents dozing quietly in the silent gloom.

The projectionist was busy elsewhere and the screen might have been silent for nearly ten minutes or more. But none of the customers had stirred.

Irene always had a damp stub of a roll-up glued to her lip. I would tell her that smoking on duty was not allowed and was thoroughly unsanitary anyway as she was selling food. Irene would roll her pink eyes at me and cough her disbelief.

'Bin doing it fer years, Mr Scur-more, never dun no 'arm to none of 'em yit.'

Irene claimed to have learned to smoke from her father who had shared his service tobacco ration with her when she was only a child.

'Durin' the Kaiser's war, that was,' she reminisced to me by way of explanation, 'long time gone nah-days. Drove a cab 'e did, arter the war, like. Used ter drive me into the Royal Hotel sometimes, win I was a chambermaid. Felt a right proper princess I did, comin' ter werk in a cab in the early morning like that. The other girls'd laugh, coz they wuz jealous-like, see?'

By the merest chance we were once able to help Irene in an unexpected way. One day young Gavin asked me if he could have a word in private. He came along to the office within the hour. I asked him in and said he could shut the door if he wished. He seemed pleased to do so. Evidently, we were to have a serious conversation. Gavin sat in the chair looking embarrassed. He took a breath and reported that he'd seen Irene's payslip quite by accident when it had dropped out of her handbag onto the staffroom floor. He said that, at a very quick glance, it looked to him as though she was paying a lot of tax and wondered if there had been a mistake. I felt rather shocked. In my experience details of pay are one of the few universally acknowledged areas of extreme discretion in the workplace.

'Have you spoken to Irene about this?' I asked.

'No. I think she doesn't know much about that stuff. I thought I'd mention it to you.' He looked at me, shifting in the chair.

'Well, that's probably a good thing. I'll look into it, certainly. You have been very discreet already, so I'll not need to remind you to continue to say as little about this as possible. Will I?'

Gavin looked at me steadily, but without challenge. He knew as well as I did that what he had reported could be very embarrassing – not to say poisonously divisive – if repeated in the wrong place and time.

'No. Right. Well, can I go then?'

'Oh, certainly. And thank you,' I ended rather lamely.

Calculating out the weekly cash pay packets was a duty I shared by turn with Miss Kaitlin every week. For myself, I simply followed the firm's procedural routine without reflection whenever I did it. Computation has always been an almost absent skill for me. Without the aid of a calculator I have to more or less guess at the proper amount for service on a restaurant bill. In calculating those vital wage figures every other week, I had been focussed mainly on mathematical accuracy. I used the pages of the government's issued weekly taxable pay tables to calculate correctly all the deductions. This was a company house rule.

Taking down the big ring binder that held the current staff pay records, I looked up Irene's records for the past year, thinking that at her age she should be on a very low taxable rate. It was very discomforting to see that she indeed appeared to be on a very high, un-coded emergency rate. Thus Irene had been incurring a weekly deduction for income tax and national insurance that was very far in excess of what she should have been paying. This appeared to have been going on for some years. I checked with Miss Kaitlin as soon as I could, and she agreed that, on reflection, there did appear to have been a possible oversight.

I telephoned the tax office and, in a lengthy consultation, cited Irene's age, tax code, and extended record of continuous payments. Over the next months there were several more calls, and then photocopies of documents to be submitted. Being cautious, I had not stressed to Irene exactly what I hoped to achieve with all this but referred vaguely to irregularities that were not her fault.

But the day came when an envelope came into the cinema from the Inland Revenue which contained two items: a letter in undiluted official-ese and a printed government cheque for several hundred pounds of refunded tax payments for Irene. I rang Miss Kaitlin at home. We agreed that I should do the happy hand-over as soon as ever might be. Accordingly, later that day, I called Irene into the office, closed the door and put the letter into her hand, wearing a big smile. She stared at the official brown envelope and blinked. She handed it straight back and said, scowling:

'I ain't dun nuffin. Yer can't sack me, yer only the assistant, Mr Scur-more.'

My heart jumped. My comfortable smug feeling of doing good for the needy melted instantly away.

'Oh Irene – I'm sorry. The letter's not bad news. Not at all. You remember I was asking you a while ago about exactly when you started here and your exact birthday and so on…?' I gave Irene my most encouraging smile.

'Yis,' said Irene, very guardedly.

'Well,' I plunged on, 'I don't know how it's happened but you have been paying too much tax to the government out of your weekly pay for quite a long time. I've been writing and telephoning them almost every week or so for the past four months, and now somebody senior at Inland Revenue has agreed with Miss Kaitlin and me and sent us back some money for you. Your money. Quite a lot of money, actually.'

I held the stupid brown envelope out towards her again.

'Is it a raise, then?' Irene asked, but now without the former angry stare.

'No, it's a one-time only refund,' I replied, flustered. 'But there will be what seems like a raise from next week because you will be paying almost no tax at all.'

'No more tax?' said she doubtfully, still not taking the envelope.

'Well, hardly any, and so about nine extra pounds every week, for you.'

'How much is in there, then?' she asked quietly, finally taking the envelope and holding it in front of her.

'Nearly six hundred and fifty pounds,' I replied, beaming like a child who has recited a long and difficult poem correctly.

'Go on. It's never that much. Can't be, can it? S'not thick enough for all that money, is it?'

'It's a cheque, Irene. You can take it to the bank.'

'Nah! Buncha thieves. I don't hold with givin' my money ter foreigners. Never! Under the floorboards, that's the ticket.' Irene was grinning at me. Could she hear my brain whirring, I wondered?

I asked a question: 'Irene, do you ever put money in the post office? You know – for Christmas or a rainy day, or whatever?' She looked rueful.

'Sometimes. Not al'us easy, is it?'
'But you do have a post-office book?'

'Yis. But I don't do it so much nowadays. Not since that nice Mr Elphick retired down to the sea. Bin stampin' my book for years, he 'ad, then he retires. Wasn't the same, sum'ow.'

Irene gazed at me with emphasis, her eyes lit with a reminiscent scorn. Clearly, she thought of retirement as something that happened only to the foolish like going out in the rain without a hat.

'Well, take that cheque to the post office with your post office bank book. Any post office. They'll give you the cash, if that's what you want.'

Irene still looked decidedly doubtful as she tottered away.

The next Friday I was handed out the weekly pay packets from the office safe as the staff came on duty. Irene grinned broadly at me as she signed for hers.

'That was a good turn yer done me an' no mistake, Mr Scurmore. Awl 'at tax money whut yer guv me. Still can't 'ardly b'leeve it.' She smoothed her unfeasible hair and smiled again. I was embarrassed, again.

'I'm pleased you got it at last. But I didn't give it to you, you know. It was yours all the time. It got lost for a while, because of a muddle.'

But from then every Friday Irene always flashed me a grateful smile on payday.

I did think to recommend to Miss Kaitlin that Gavin be given a promotion when a slot occurred in the future. I was saddened a year or two later to hear on the company grapevine that he had not turned up for work one day. And no more was ever seen or heard of him.

The Moulin was not the most demanding of posts, and I was not very inclined to be too specific about what kind of cinema it was or where it was located whenever kind relatives or friends ever affected surprise and pleasure on learning from my mother that 'Nick had now been promoted to a cinema in the West End'. A time was to come when I would be a little less coy, but that was yet to be.

At the Moulin there were seasonal disruptions to our collective somnambulism. Along with the rest of Soho we always did very brisk business in the first week of December. The annual Royal Smithfield Show took place at the Earl's Court Arena back then. The Smithfield Grand Prize is the supreme achievement that a livestock farmer can aspire to. There is a lively week of competitions and trade fairs leading up to the final event. And in the evenings many of the farmers feel that they must visit the famed diversions of Soho that legend and gossip have long evoked. Probably as an aperitif to more physical pleasures, clusters of men and boys in ties and waxed jackets would sometimes give the Moulin's 'uncensored' joys a try. Within an hour or so most would emerge and plunge off down the street towards the restaurants and the battered doorways next to them. Doors that stood open to the street, on the jamb of which would be pinned several small paper cards that might read some variant on 'French Model, 1st Floor'. From the street the passing punter could clearly see within to the flight of grubby wooden stairs that led up to a very sublunary heaven.

The Eros on the corner of Shaftesbury Avenue and Piccadilly Circus, 1979

Housed under street level of the Monaco Building, the art deco style Eros News Theatre opened in 1934. The site was so tight on space that the projection booth was in the building next door. It was operated by the Capitol and Provincial News Theatres which later became the Classic Cinema chain. When newsreels ceased to be produced in the 1950s, it became the Classic Cartoon Cinema. It operated as the Eros, showing adult films, from 1976 to 1985. The building was subsequently used for retail.

Klaus Hiltscher

https://www.flickr.com/photos/khiltscher

The Eros Cinema, Piccadilly Circus
Summer 1982

The Eros Cinema, a sister house within the company, stood less than a hundred yards from the Moulin. The Eros was, to my mind, a sadder and more dejected place than even the Moulin. In the 1930s and 40s the Eros had probably been something of a flagship of the news reel cinemas. It literally faced Piccadilly Circus, and the pavement directly outside was, pre-Covid, one of the most trodden in Europe. Crowds surged around that narrow corner for twenty hours in every twenty-four. So the Eros News Cinema, in its days of glory as much as in its sad present, was perfectly placed to be a respite for tired shoppers, dilatory commuters, and unimaginative tourists for hour after hour.

The paybox was a little cubicle that had a curved glass front facing into the street in the classical manner. It was veneered in worn mahogany with the faintest traces of gilt paint still to be seen on the few rococo curlicues of carving that remained. Beyond was a narrow entrance into a cramped little curved vestibule that was still fitted with gilt-edged mirrors, all very smoked and rubbed. (Refurbished, those mirrors would have been the pride and joy of the ladies' changing rooms in some retro-fitted boutique in Spitalfields today.) On the left there was a doorway, curtained in rubbed, much-handled red velvet, that led into the stalls seating of the lower hall.

The Eros had been designed to have an upper circle from the beginning. Accordingly, an elegant staircase had been fitted into the tall narrow volume of the foyer. A neatly curved set of steps led around and up to the left. The stair handrail was made of gold-painted cast iron, very light but strong. The iron uprights of the bannister had been fashioned into figures to suggest cinema news-crews that were shown perched on the roofs of their vans, filming the world's wonders that you were now just about to view for yourself. Some of the uprights also suggested cameras and klieg lights and directors in jodhpurs and flat caps, in fact the full iconography of old Hollywood. That balustrade was a true beauty of execution: neat, evocative, functional, pretty. It was also rubbed and worn and mostly grey from long, long use. It reminded me of Oscar Wilde's tale of the gold-plated statue of the prince that is stripped of all its beauties of gold leaf and jewelled eyes by the uncaring townsfolk. Upstairs was a small, curved auditorium circle of red velvet seats. Looking down into the stall seats below it was clear that the whole place had been planned as a half-size version of one of the big Shaftesbury Avenue theatres. There was even mahogany and gilt framing around the screen itself, though the colour had quite vanished, save for a few vestigial traces. By now the elegant Eros had sunk very low, playing the same barely coherent smutty trash as the Moulin, to the same barely coherent audience.

Late one very warm evening in July 1982, I was dozing at my desk, head on forearms. It had been an unusually slow night for a Saturday. The Eros had no air-conditioning, of course, and it was very close indoors. There was only forty minutes to go to 12.40am and the end of the show. The small and very dirty window that looked down into Piccadilly Circus was open wide to let in a little of the refreshing night fumes, while the soft but constant surf-roar of traffic aided my slumbers. Suddenly the steady blur of noise changed to a cacophony of claxons and yelling. I jerked awake. Had there been a multiple pile-up? A sudden arson attack? I lurched to the window.

Below was an amazing sight: perhaps thirty cars, and nearly as many motorbikes and scooters were all circulating around and around Piccadilly Circus, swinging hysterically round the statue of Eros at the centre of the square, all tooting and blaring away at once.

The occupants were no calmer, all of them waving and ululating with vigour. What was this madness? The drivers were all men and most of the passengers too. But then, looking more carefully, I could see there was a sprinkling of women amongst this joyous carousel. They were all wearing headscarves. Matching striped headscarves. How quaint. And now finally I noticed the flags that bore the same colours as the headscarves – the flags of green and white and red tied to the door handles, to the radio masts, to the necks or waists or even wrists of many of the men driving. And the ululations were becoming more sustained now: 'Italia, Italia, champione della mondo', 'Italia – ITEEETAL-EEE-AAAAH'. Finally the truth was borne to my dull Saxon mind. This was the end of the World Cup – Italy had just demonstrated conclusively that it was the greatest soccer-playing nation in all the world. Italy had won, and now every restaurateur and waiter and violin-maker and tailor and waitress in Soho were shouting their nation's praises to London's rooftops. The festival caravan at last began to branch off down Piccadilly towards Green Park. Throughout the night there was to be a lively rear-guard that followed in disorderly sections, but the noise was definitely less.

I was just gathering my thoughts when Andy, the Eros' ancient doorman, tapped on the office door. 'There's a problem in the circle. There's a naked man, Sir. In the circle, Sir.'

This obviously made no sense. 'No, Andy, it's just a lot of Italians – they've won the World Cup, I think. Just celebrating.'
He looked worried. 'No, Sir. Really – in the circle, there's a naked man.'

'Seriously?' I asked, still very befuddled. Andy nodded his grey head. I thought I'd better attend to this mystery.

Down the narrow back stairs I tottered, with Andy following behind, and stepped round the worn velvet curtain, entering the circle. On the screen two outstandingly healthy young women were in a hotel bedroom giggling and undressing each other. So far, so normal. It was stiflingly warm. There was the usual scattering of single blokes slumped in their seats. Andy and I walked quietly along the curved aisle at the back of the circle. Andy pointed and hissed in my ear,

'That's him, there.'

He stood back, respectful of my authority. I stepped down three rows and turned into the row behind. I didn't want to get too close. I thought I could hear tittering behind me. Surely not. I could see the back of the man's head silhouetted against the screen's light. Some pattern balding. And nude shoulders. Now that was a little uncommon. The man was middle-aged and sitting calmly, watching Fifi and Olga continue their mutual explorations.

From behind I leaned forward slightly. The gentleman was indeed as naked as when he was born. He had his hands crossed domestically over his belly. His clothes were all folded into a neat pile on the seat beside him. I leaned forward slightly and whispered into his nearside ear in my best managerial whisper,

'Sir, the film is ending very soon. It's nearly time to go home.'

He glanced round at me and now I saw his face. I was almost disappointed. He was not the Phantom of the Opera nor Mrs Norman Bates. He was, instead, Mr Home Counties commuter, 1943 model. He had a neat grey moustache. He gazed at me mildly. The giggling several rows behind us was starting up again.

'The film is going to end very soon,' I repeated. 'The lights will all come on. Don't you think you'd better be putting your clothes back on?'

The gentleman looked mildly taken aback, exactly as if I was a train conductor insisting he give up his reserved seat. However, he nodded. I stepped away back down the row. To my immense relief I could see he was starting to climb into his underwear.

'Andy, watch him – I'll go get the door chains. Stay here and bang on the cleaner's lights as soon as the credits roll. Follow him out if need be. Yeah?'

But in ten minutes more the house was clear, the doors chained, and we were all on our way home.

The months flew on, routinely. But there was a signifying moment. One early evening the following spring I was on duty at the front of the Moulin. It was a damp, chilly night, still dark at 7.00pm, with the lights on the Shaftesbury Avenue theatres twinkling away down at the end of the street. Nearer to hand the smell of the neighbouring kosher salt beef bar was blowing into the Moulin's doors. Behind me came a sudden crashing of feet as four young men blundered out through the doors, shouldering me aside.

'S'fuckin' shit, yoor films,' one of them bellowed back into the foyer as he slipped past. 'I got tapes that's fuckin' much harden 'n 'at shit at 'ome.'

He glared at us all, his voice indignantly rising on the final word. That his own home could disturb his sleep far more vigorously than the famed naughtiness of Soho's films was clearly an outrage. Of course he was announcing the end of the cosily shabby world of the Moulin and all shows like it, little though any of us understood it at the time. Porn film distributors were already recognising the value of the now rapidly emerging VHS home video market, quicker than most of the bigger distributors, and certainly quicker than any legislators. And indeed, within another five years halls like the Moulin would vanish almost entirely away.

The next morning, back at the Moulin, there was a surprise. Mr Brown came in quite unannounced and commanded an audience with me in Miss Kaitlin's office. She was already behind her desk, expectant. Mr Brown dropped himself into the only other chair. He looked at me very directly. I stood there wondering. I was to go to head office later that afternoon. Stuart Hall, the head of all cinema programming, both London and nationally, wanted to see me.

Press launch of the Premiere Cinema on Shaftesbury Avenue, March 1984.

From L to R, Front-of-House Manager Nick Scudamore, Yoram Globus, Manager George McCann, Stuart Hall, Menahem Golan, Barry Jenkins, unidentified. Golan and Globus were the new owners of the Cannon-Classic chain.

The basement cinema, known as The Columbia when it opened in 1959, was renamed the Premiere at this date. It has had three screens since 1998 and is now known as the Curzon, Soho.

PSA Communications

The Cannon Classic Cinema, Shaftesbury Avenue Spring 1983

There is a fable about a newly appointed regional commissar travelling, late in 1918, into the farthest reaches of the Ural Mountains. After several hard weeks on horseback he arrives, with his wind-blown pony caravan, at the regional hamlet from where he will begin the actual practicalities of bringing the glorious new Soviet Socialist Revolution to this rural backwater. He enters the local inn and commands a room and a bath and a bed. The innkeeper is cheery and curious,

'You are welcome, Exalted Sir. We get few travellers from Moscow here. We did hear tell of a bit of a political disturbance in Moscow in October last year. Can you please tell us, your Eminence, who won?'

Head office for the whole Classic Cinema chain was only three hundred yards away from the Moulin up Wardour Street. Despite its physical proximity, head office itself and all its edicts might as well have been as distant from us as if they had indeed been sent from Moscow. In fact, Classic Cinemas had recently just been through a similar comprehensive revolution and was only now reconstituting itself. The whole Classic Cinema chain had been bought out by Cannon Films International. Cannon was a rapidly expanding foreign film production house that had built its huge success by making imitation American-style films which they then sold throughout the Middle East and into African and Asian territories. Cannon had been mining the tropes of the American-derived action genres, in particular the Rambo and Robocop franchises, as well as those of American Graffiti and related teen comedies, in order to present very similar popular films to non-English-speaking audiences, but always made with very much lower budgets. When you remember that in many parts of the world the original American films would have been entirely dubbed for the same local audiences, the success of the trick is less surprising.

The two owners of Cannon Films were a pair of Israeli cousins, Menahem Golan and Yoram Globus, who wanted to bring their films to Europe, with their eye on establishing themselves, in the future, as a full-on studio making films actually in Hollywood. Right now they were in the process of reorganising sleepy Classic Cinemas, and their first intent was to use the cinema chain as a duct through which to pour the films with which they had already had successes elsewhere into British popular culture.

But first I was to meet Stuart Hall. He was one of the few survivors from the old guard at Classic Cinemas, after a reputedly sanguinary clear out of Classic's top management. Stuart had been programming for the whole national chain for a number of years. His job had been to decide exactly when films would be planned to arrive in local Classic cinemas and to give the final okay as to when they would be moved from one auditorium to another or dropped or transferred elsewhere. He was a pale-skinned, dapper man, with manicured nails and very carefully styled hair. He wore a habitual expression of one who has just smelled something unpleasant. Evidently I smelled no better than the rest of humanity. His proposition to me was a strange one: Cannon-Classic had newly acquired the lease of a big first-run cinema on Shaftesbury Avenue. It was a top-of-the-line flagship theatre. He was looking for a suitable person to be a front-of-house manager there but with particular responsibilities for running one-off special programmes – press shows, sneak previews and the like. In addition, such a person would be expected to plan and programme late-night film shows of his own devising. Was I interested?

On the face of it this was a big step up – it had actual creative potential of a kind that cinema management, in its traditional form, does not. To move on from the worn and grubby environment of the Moulin and the Eros to a flagship hall: that would be something in itself. There was to be a pay rise too. A small one admittedly, but a rise is a rise. Stuart Hall concluded by saying that I should have to present some scheduling ideas for upcoming art-house releases – that I would probably have to give a presentation with some dummy titles to the management board. Could I attend head office again at 10.00am next Monday? I was alarmed, excited, fearful and exultant. And accepted all his conditions on the spot.

In those days it was common knowledge within the company that I spent much of my leisure time in other cinemas watching as many films as I could – and nearly all my leave at film festivals. What Mr Hall didn't know was that I had all the programmes of the most recent New York and Los Angeles and Paris and London film festivals at home and resolved to make up a dummy programme with pages torn from all of them – and then suggest the least *outré* titles to the board the following Monday. I really had very little idea what I was getting into or how much influence I would really have, but I had nothing to lose and much to gain from behaving confidently and pretending to far more competence than I actually possessed. Leaving head office I walked the short distance back through Soho to the Moulin.

My brain was flicking through fashionable directors: Fassbinder, Oshima, Wenders, Olmi, Ken Russell, Coppola, Tarkovsky. I'd need to get my one and only suit dry-cleaned. Where could I use a photocopier? Could I get my best black brogues repaired in time? A haircut? It was like planning an emergency wedding.

As I approached Miss Kaitlin's door I tried to compose my face to look less hysterical. She was bent over a ledger. She looked up and raised her eyebrows, 'So?' In as even a tone as I could manage, I said, 'I'm to move to the new house on Shaftesbury Avenue. Front-of-house stuff. Bit of programming as well.' She smiled warmly.

'Ah. So Stuart wasn't exaggerating. I didn't think you'd be here long. Careful though – you'll be swimming in very dirty water over there. But I'm pleased for you.'

I felt very relieved – sometimes an assistant manager leaving a post suddenly can be a bit traumatic for a manager and I was grateful for Miss Kaitlin's diplomacy.

I went to the library the next morning and photocopied the pages of the foreign film festival programmes. Then I went back to the flat and sat in Martha's kitchen rearranging the loose pages into a preferred order to create the faux programme leaflet of my own devising. I then stapled the loose sheets together to make four separate copies. This odd creation was to be my principal prop at the upcoming meeting. One for Barry Jones, the new CEO whom Golan and Globus had parachuted into the company, two more for whoever looked like they might need it, and finally one copy for me to busk my presentation from.

I went for a long walk that Sunday. I had the day off, and Martha and Ray would be at home breakfasting late and reading the papers, so I wanted to be out and walking and planning my pitch. I've always found walking a great spur to creative preparation: the rhythm of my own steps means I can hear better how the words flow and then calculate more accurately the best sequence for the ideas that I intend to use to support my thesis. From the flat I walked down to Regent's Canal. It was a beautiful crisp spring mid-morning – the trees throwing their leaves gently into the wind like offerings; the sky huge and blue above, with the clouds high and sailing westward slowly. The canal walkway was well populated. I passed the brightly coloured well-wrapped babies of the well-to-do in expensive pushchairs with mums and dads in full attendance, all enjoying their weekly walk as a threesome; happy dogs tugging their owners along; pairs of lovers, both types: some pairs of lovers are always twined round each other and gazing as much at each other as they are at their surroundings while they murmur together; the other type walk quietly, hand-in-hand in companionable silence. Bicycles whirred by, sometimes in family clusters, all wearing matching helmets – they looked like the duck families on the canal, in uniform and in single file. My brain was spinning smoothly, and I felt very happy. Whatever came of tomorrow's trial, at least I was to be given some kind of an unusual chance to show what I could do.

Towards the end of the afternoon I walked home to the flat. Feeling expansive, and hungry, I stopped for some fish and chips. When I got in it was full dark. The flat was warm and comfy and smelled of roast meat. Martha's front room was aglow with soft lights, and she and Ray were both slouched in soft chairs, the Sunday papers littered around them. I gave a wave as I passed the open sitting-room door, only three steps more into my bedroom. Martha waved back, smiling. She beckoned me in and pointed at my newish toy – the VHS player under her TV. Video-players were not then as ubiquitous as they would soon become. Indeed they were still so expensive to buy that I rented mine from a hire-firm.

'What you got in your player, Nick? Anything we can all enjoy?'

I introduced them to *Hill Street Blues* that evening. This was the newest TV cop-show hot from the States. It was in the traditional one-hour drama segments but was otherwise radical in form: the story lines did not always play out to a pat conclusion; sometimes the cops were just plain wrong; there were a lot of Black and Hispanic faces, and not just in comedy roles. The less glossy look of most of the actors on the show was reinforced, in the writing, by a real sense of the imminent collapse of the very damaged urban environment which all the characters inhabited. HSB was very novel and refreshingly dark for an American network TV drama. So the three of us sat and laughed at the jokes and groaned at the dramas and had a very happy evening together.

In the morning I shaved and trimmed back my beard neatly. The Italian suit looked okay, even flattering. I ate breakfast properly. It felt just like those mornings when you went to school as usual but this particular morning to sit a three-hour written exam for which you had spent the whole of the previous term preparing. In Wardour Street I walked into the company head-office foyer for only the second time. The brunette receptionist behind the curved desk gave me a bored appraisal as she rang Stuart Hall's number. She jerked her chin at me as she dropped the phone onto its cradle.

'He's comin' dahn,' she promised.

In two minutes Stuart appeared, wearing a bright tie and a pink fitted shirt with white collar and cuffs. He smiled me the thinnest of smiles.

'Morning. Follow me.'

The corners of his mouth curved down again immediately. He turned away briskly and I followed his quick lope up the stairs to the first floor. We stopped outside a pair of double doors. They were tall and wide and expensively veneered. Stuart pushed the nearest one open without ceremony and then shoved me into the room and, coming behind, closed it firmly shut. The effect was like one of those unsettling cuts in a Welles or Polanski drama. A dozen or more faces, all of them utter strangers to me, stared at the new face propelled so unceremoniously into their midst.

They sat round a vast oval table made of some dark wood. No one spoke. Stuart marched me up to the head of the table. He said, 'Barry Jones, I want you to meet Nick Scudamore,' and he stepped back.

Barry Jones had quick attentive eyes, and his handshake was smooth, even and brief. 'So you're the new wonder-boy?' he said looking me all the way down and then all the way up again, from shoes to haircut. I was trying to think of the best way to respond to this for the benefit of the whole audience around the table when he continued, 'So you're like me then. I've only been here four weeks, and this lot are still waiting to see what I'll do next. Want to show us what you've got, Nick?'

I took a deep breath and reminded the assembled greybeards of what it was I had been asked to do – to concoct a plausible dummy programme of films for the new first-release art-house that Cannon-Classic had recently acquired. This playlist was presented without reference to whatever the actual acquisition costs might be, as this was well outside my expertise. I read my list of films: Fassbinder, Olmi, Wenders, Chabrol, Lelouch, Oshima, Allen, Coppola etc, etc and outlined the plots and named the stars for each film, two minutes on each.

I got to the end and stopped and looked round the room. No one looked at me. They all looked at Barry. He looked at me and said: 'Impressive, Nick. There's enough titles there to take us through the next nine months, at least. But I think you'd better leave us now.'

And he turned back to the table with a straight mouth and his eyebrows rising.

Outside in the corridor I had no idea what to do. I decided to wait ten minutes and then leave. Anyone who needed me would know how and where to find me. Since I effectively now had the day off I decided to walk up to the new cinema where I would be working in only a few more days and have a look around. The place might be all locked up – or there might be an advance party of Classic's team of geriatric decorators. In fact the team usually consisted only of old Ralfie who worked mostly on his own. Ralfie had endeared himself to me by remarking one early morning, as he stretched a bit of cheap fabric over one of the most worn of the chairs at the Eros,

'Ah, well; one good wet fart and it'll be buggered agin.'

The new cinema was only ten minutes away up Shaftesbury Avenue, opposite the fire station. The cinema's entrance was the entire retail frontage on the ground floor. Above that was a smart five-storey office-block. I believe that rents from the offices had been used by the original owners to subsidise the running expenses of the cinema. The standard of construction and decoration was superb, far grander than anything Cannon-Classic had previously operated. The hall itself was subterranean, reached via two flights of wide steps. There were lacquered wooden panels along all the walls in blond oak, a beautiful burnished steel handrail on the stairs, top-quality carpeting throughout. The ceiling and wall lights appeared to be custom-made fitments of wood, dark brass, and smoked glass. The effect suggested space, elegance and comfort whilst disguising the reality of descending deep underground into an artificial space necessarily lit without any reference to daylight. The suggestion was of a windowless corridor that might run along the rows of burnished wooden doors of the first-class cabins on a super-luxury cruise liner.

The auditorium itself was stunning. The back wall of the hall proper was curved and gave a 130-degree aspect towards the screen at the far end. This back wall was lined at the top with the same wooden panels as on the stairs, but at shoulder height a rich blue carpet began below the panels and then flowed downwards and out onto the floor of the hall, like a warm river of dark wool. This would also serve to absorb some of the sound from the large speakers at the front of the hall. There were narrow cream columns supporting the roof, very carefully placed so that the sightlines were hardly affected at all. In gentle curves arcing away from the screen were over 500 very comfortable seats covered in a dark blue velveteen. They sat on the warm blue carpet in a complementary shade of a richer and darker blue. Instead of a curtain the screen was bathed in a soft glow of carefully adjusted theatre lights. The whole effect was lushly hospitable. Expensive, but understated. It was a room in which to have a treat.

The technical side was excellent despite being definitely pre-digital and even pre-Dolby. The projectors were the rarely seen old-fashioned carbon-arcs that burned a rather brighter and steadier light than conventional projector bulbs. Carbon-arcs were notoriously labour-intensive to operate, but always threw a superb light through the projector lens towards the screen. The whole place, from the street doors to the projection suite, had been designed and built to a standard rather than to a price.

None of the decoration in the public area was new; all of it had seen a good twenty years' service to the public already. But because the original specifications had been so very high the deterioration was only now becoming apparent. For example, the gentlemen's urinal, a beautiful ten-foot wall of marble and brass in a late deco style, tended to pong. This rather spoiled the effect of the gleaming washbasins and brass towel rails and mahogany-veneered cubicle doors of the toilet stalls. The ladies' remained fresher overall, but then they often do.

The manager's office was behind a heavy door with lovely, veneered marquetry around it. The door itself suggested the entrance to the presidential suite of a very grand hotel. The office within was rectangular and the size of Martha's whole sitting room at least. It was wallpapered in pale blue and gold and had a big fake Chippendale desk and two straight chairs, one plonked in front of the desk. The walls were bare save for business charts that had been pinned to the wallpaper behind the desk. Behind it sat a dapper small man. He looked up as I walked into his office that first morning. 'Yes?'

'I'm Nick Scudamore.'

'Indeed. And how can I help you, Mr Scudamore?' There was a soft drawl of Edinburgh in his voice.

'Ah, well, um, Stuart Hall has sent me to join the team here.'

There was a rather painful pause.

'Stuart Hall – at Classic cinemas,' I urged hopefully.

He stood up. He was wearing a beautifully brushed three-piece soft grey flannel suit. He was indeed a short man, and rather round in the front. His hair was sparse but well cut, and his shoes were a polished gleam. He raised his grey eyebrows.

'I know who he is,' said the man softly but firmly, 'but...?' he invited.

'I'm to be the new Assistant Manager here, I believe,' I said weakly, feeling very foolish now.

'Are you now?' said the grey-suited one, still very quietly. 'Are you now, indeed? Well, perhaps I'll give Mr Stuart Hall a call.'

He glanced at a thin gold wristwatch as he sat back down in his desk chair. He picked up the receiver of one of the pair of telephones on his desk and motioned me into the straight chair opposite. I really wanted to leave, but I sat.

He dialled. 'Yes, good morning. George McCann here at the Soho. Yes, the new one, yes. Can I speak to Mr Stuart Hall please? I see. Really. When do you expect him back? Really.

Well, have him call me as soon as he can, won't you, please? Thank you.'

His voice trilled upwards dismissively on the last words. He sat back in his chair and gave me a considered look.

'Mr Hall has said not a word about an assistant to me,' said he, looking at me very directly. This was a moment to be frank.

'I'm very embarrassed,' I said. 'I've made a stupid mistake. I've just come from Wardour Street. Stuart Hall took me into a meeting with Barry Jones, and since they didn't seem to need me anymore, I thought I'd come here and have a look around.' Now he smiled a soft smile, his eyes suddenly attentive.

'Ah – so you've met the new boss, have ye? That's a wonder, to be sure it is. There's many of us would relish the chance to meet our new lord and master. So you've met Mr Barry Jones already. And then you thought you'd bring yourself here, did ye? Well, now. You're a curious one, aren't you? So tell me, Mr Scudamore, what do you think of the place, then?'

This was easy. I said how much I liked the quality of the build and the fit-out, the elegance of the lines of sight in the hall, the superb throw, the softness of the carpets, the obviously high level of maintenance, the bespoke light fittings, the beautiful panelling along all the walls, the marquetry on the doors, the modern look throughout, even though the place was not brand-new. I went on for quite five minutes. The man opposite leaned back behind his desk, his smile widening as I spoke on. By the end his expression was almost mischievous.

'Aye, there are a few nice points about the place, to be sure. And a guid class of folk who attend, by all accounts. And we've the Royal Room, o'course. Have ye seen it, the Royal Room?' he asked with a quiet eagerness. I had no idea to what he might be referring.

'Aye, 'tis a wonder, the Royal Room.' He stood up decisively. 'I'm George McCann, the manager.'

He stuck out his hand. I stood and shook his outstretched hand. George gave me a real smile now.

'Come on then,' he invited, and skipped round his big desk and towards the door. I followed and he led me back downstairs towards the auditorium.

On the floor below his office, directly opposite the entrance doors to the vast auditorium, was a smart-looking veneered door without any marquetry to draw attention to it. There was no handle on the outside either, only a keyhole. George pulled a large bunch of keys from his pocket and selected a key. The lock turned with a solid click. George swung the door open and flicked the light switch. Within was a rectangular room, a panelled windowless chamber. There was a small period side-desk against one wall. Above it was a large framed mirror. Against the two further walls were a pair of large sofas covered in now rather faded chintz. In the middle of the room two large matching easy chairs huddled, rather uneasily, next to a circular drinks table. Against each of the four walls stood a matching table lamp on a bespoke stand, one including a telephone. The room's wall panels had been carefully varnished to a blonde lustre. The dark blue carpeting familiar from the auditorium now had an additional narrow gold border. The effect was, in truth, a little faded, but still sumptuous. George McCann pointed to a narrow door in the far wall. 'Tidy little washbasin and er, the other facilities, y'know?' The whole arrangement was clearly intended for the private comfort of grandees who might be attending a screening but who could not possibly be expected to wait in public view. It was a VIP lounge from an era when people who entered such domains had achieved the privilege by something more than accumulated air-miles. (Later on I, having neither entitlement nor air-miles, was to become rather wont to let myself in for a quiet kip in my off-hours.)

George and I turned and went back up the stairs to his office. I felt I had been shown something that represented almost a personal treasure for George, so I was as intrigued as he was pleased at having shown it off. We sat down again in his office.

'Will ye stay for a quick cup of tea, Mr Scudamore?'

'If I'm not imposing on your time, I'd be delighted,' I said, because I was. George dismissed any notion of imposition with a friendly shrug.

'Ah no. Now then, are there any biscuits, I'm wondering...?'

As he looked round the room his hands were picking up a packet of rather expensive-looking cigarettes from the desk. There was a large ashtray that had two or three butts in it already. I now noticed that the tips of his left hand fingers were faintly stained a pale yellow. His eyes cast quietly about the room.

'There are always biscuits,' he mused aloud, 'but I can never find where that woman hides them. Mrs Robinson is nay on duty as of yet. She'll be another half an hour ar' more, I'm sorry to say.' But he didn't seem perturbed.

He rose, perhaps to go in search of tea or biscuits or even both, when one of the phones on his desk rang.

'George McCann here. Ah, good morning, Stuart. Yes. Yes, he is, as a matter of fact. Yes. Already, yes. Oh, just having a good look round.' George smiled across at me. Then his tone changed. He listened hard, frowning. 'Really? What, now? Both of them? And Mr Jones too? Well, are ye coming, then? I should hope so – this could be a wee bit tricky, y'know? I'm aware of that, Stuart. Well, in half an hour then.'

George looked across at me.

'They are coming here to have a look at the place, and at yourself, I shouldn't wonder; Mr Jones as well as Mr Golan and Mr Globus. In half an hour. We'd better get ready.'

George looked rather strained. I felt only panic. He went on 'They've never been here before. They'll be wanting a walk round I suppose, and I've only had the keys to the place for four days – it's nay tidy enow fer a grand visit. Have you been in the box yet? Did you see Mike or Henry? Oh, bother.'

I replied that at least one of the projectionists must be on site because the door to the box had been open when I had peeped in earlier.

'That's as well,' George replied. 'Go see if you can find either one of them. Tell them who you are and tell 'em that Mr McCann says there's to be a full visit from Head Office in twenty-five minutes and they are to make ready as best they can. And to put on a tie as well. The full drill.'

It was my turn to skip out of the room now. I nipped back along the corridor to the heavy door at the other end that was still propped open with a fire extinguisher. I looked into the projection suite. The pair of huge projectors stood silent. The floor was swept, the shelves filled with neatly stacked workroom paraphernalia. Then the fire door beyond the machines eased open slightly, and a fit youngish man folded himself neatly back into the room, his right arm making a final throwing gesture as he slipped in. Evidently a cigarette break had recently concluded.

He saw me lurking just inside the door. The young man grudgingly admitted to being Mike, the assistant projectionist. I gave him my name and Mr McCann's news. Mike looked doubtful on both counts.

'You could ring him on the house phone to check,' I suggested.

'Are you alone today?' Mike looked resentful.

'Chief'll be here in half an hour. What did you say your name was again?'

I told him again. He nodded, more attentively this time.

'I'll tell Henry as soon as he gets in,' he said.

Back in the office George was pulling a lot of the papers off his desk and piling them randomly on top of one of the filing cabinets.

'We'll need to offer them something,' I said. 'I'll make the tea if you'll show me where the kettle is.'

George looked up. He nodded and pulled open a drawer in the desk. He searched for a moment, reaching towards the back of the drawer. He straightened up and passed me a heavy bunch of keys, looking red-faced and a bit breathless.

'Haven't time to go through them with you now. There's a staff area behind the sales stand along this floor. Let yourself in and do the best you can. Be quick, now.' George turned back to the desk.

I went back down the corridor. My heart was beating fast. It felt like that moment in the final ten minutes when the villain leaves the dungeon as he announces 'Zere, Mr Bond. Ze bomb is primed. You 'ave exactly eight minutes to escape from zose 'andcuffs. High ham a compassionate man, no?' and we get a snap close-up of red digits on the bomb ticking backwards. At the end of the corridor, opposite the projection suite door – now firmly closed – was a smaller door. It took me a full minute to find the right key and then to insert and turn it.

Inside the sales kiosk I could see a further door. This door led back into a small room all neatly fitted out with shelves, a small fridge and a kitchen counter. There was also a standard aluminium moulded sink set above a pair of cupboards. And a kettle. There were biscuits of three varieties in another cupboard above, as well as an unmatched selection of chipped and indifferently cleaned mugs. In two minutes I had the kettle boiling, the five least chipped mugs a little cleaner and ready for use, a saucer of biscuits, and a jug charged with milk from the fridge. Now I had to find a tray. A quick look up, down, around. There didn't seem to be one. I did find an unvarnished piece of broken floorboard leaning against the end of the cabinet, however. It was almost three feet long and about nine inches wide, and when I picked it up to examine it more closely I saw that it was already imprinted with the ghosts of small circles made by earlier mugs. I gave it a hasty wipe. Bingo. We were now all set to deliver tea on demand when the grandees turned up.

I walked back down the corridor to the manager's office. George had cleared most of the papers off his desk and was wiping a not very clean cloth over the two phones. The large ashtray was still there. I took it up and looked at him. George nodded.

'Ah yes, well, you'd better take it away and give it a wee wipe over – but bring it straight back, mind. Then you'd better go upstairs and keep a lookout. We've no upstairs staff coming on for nigh on another forty minutes at least.'

When I returned a moment or so later with the ashtray, I thought the office was empty. I put the ashtray down on the desk and turned. George was looking at himself in a small mirror fixed to the wall behind the office door. He was combing his hair carefully back into position. He clearly managed what remained of his hair with great attention. He smiled very thinly as he turned round.

'Nothing sillier than an old man's vanity, hey?' he said in a dry whisper.

'Got to look respectable for the top brass?' I offered.

Now he grinned. His teeth were small, and a little yellowed from the cigarettes. Then he tugged at the bottom of his waistcoat and stood up straight. His mouth became a line.

'Better get up there. Call down the stairs when you see 'em. There's nay noise just now. I'll hear ye.'

Up at the top of the stairs I walked across the foyer to look out through the wide sheets of plate glass into Shaftesbury Avenue. The pedestrian traffic was steady but not frantic. Cannon Classic's Head Office, where I had busked my introductory presentation barely an hour ago, was only three hundred yards away inside darkest Soho. I watched the street corner carefully, expecting a posse of impressively grand folk to appear striding importantly round the corner at any moment.

Accordingly, I almost missed the gleaming black Mercedes limo, as long as a railway carriage, that pulled up alongside all of the cinema doors at the same time. The vestibule seemed darker suddenly. The far nearside door swung open, and Stuart Hall slid neatly out onto the pavement and immediately turned back to speak into the interior of the limo. I ran back to the head of the stairs and called out, 'They're HERE' down to the landing below. I turned to face the street and straightened my face as well. Through the glass swing doors came Stuart Hall leading Barry Jones, and an unshaven thickset man in a very rumpled suit. He looked as though he might have slept in it. He had a full head of greying dark hair that had not seen a comb recently. With them was a fourth man in a narrow-cut dark blue cashmere blazer which he wore over cream polo shirt and slacks.

Stuart narrowed his eyes at me very warily and almost whispered,

'Where's George?' as he looked over my shoulder.

'On his way here,' I replied evenly, not caring for the lack of a greeting or even a token introduction.

Barry Jones and the others were rotating their heads about to look up into the upper corners of the vestibule the way people often do when under an impressive new roof.

'Good morning, gentlemen. Welcome.'

It was George coming up to the head of the stairs, radiating diplomacy. He walked smoothly forward beaming professional politesse from every pore.

'Stuart…?'

'Morning, Mr McCann. Gentlemen, may I introduce Mr George McCann, the very experienced manager of our new flagship art-house cinema?'

They all formed up in a line, still looking about. Stuart now gestured towards the rumpled suit.

'George, this is Mr Menahem Golan, and…' – gesturing now towards the dark blue blazer – 'this is Mr Larry Izzard. And Mr Barry Jones has joined us here at head office, as I'm sure you know.'

Stuart Hall now stepped back behind the three of them. George stepped forward. 'Gentlemen, you are all most welcome. Can I take you on a short tour now or may I invite you into my office for some refreshments?' He looked polished and confident and hospitable.

Menahem gave a huge smile and waved both his arms proprietorially. But his eyes were not warm.

'Hah – nice place, m'be. We can see zer seats first, an zen we gotta make a call – t' Hollyvood,' he said, looking with emphasis at Larry standing there in his cream slacks.

George nodded, still welcoming, still deferential. As he led the quartet to the head of the stairs he looked at me directly and mouthed the single word: 'Tea...?'

I followed behind the delegation but turned off at the first landing below. I skipped along to the staff room kitchen and prepared the tea set out earlier. I put the five unmatched mugs and the teapot onto the tray that was really only a length of planking. Also the little jug of milk and a chipped little bowl with sugar. Not to mention the biscuits. And three spoons. The plank looked crowded. I took it up gingerly and stepped along to the open office door.

The glories of the auditorium could not have detained them long, as they were already disposing themselves around George's office. Menahem was ensconced behind George's desk, and Larry Izzard and Barry Jones were across from him. Stuart and George were each carrying one of the easy chairs towards the desk. I walked up and put the plank of teas carefully on the nearest edge of the desk. And stepped back, respectfully, like a butler. Larry was attaching something to one of the phones. Menahem was watching the process of wiring this circular device to the telephone with great attention. The two of them were both focussed on Larry's actions – as if Larry were performing a conjuring trick on the desktop for Menahem. Nobody bothered with the tea. I stood at the back next to George, and Stuart was seated beside and just slightly behind Barry. The hierarchy of command was evident again. The two men sat back from their work on the desk.

Larry looked very satisfied.

'That should do it. Niftiest gadget I ever had. Chuck Bronson loved his when I gave it to him.' Menahem waved his arms appreciatively. 'I'll get 'em for all ze offices. An' all zer branches. Whatcha tink, hey Barry?'

'Well,' said Barry, 'I'm sure they might be useful...'

At that exact moment the phone on the desk rang and Menahem made a wide grab for it. The entire plank of unwanted teas crashed to the floor as he put the receiver to his ear.

'Chuck, how you doin' man? What? What's that? Oh nuttin'. Jus' sumtin' here. So listen Chuck, whaddya tink? Ya wanna do zer picture – right?'

Charles Bronson's very distinctive growl of a voice came out of the box on the desk attached to the phone.

'Hey Menahem. Is Larry there?'

Larry leant forward immediately, ignoring his scalded ankles. 'Hi Chuck, yes I'm here in London with Menahem and we're talking about your deal on this new picture, maybe. Do you have any questions?'

From out of the box Charles Bronson growled again:

'Is the money right?'

'The regular deal.'

'Do I have to ride a horse? And the bad guys go down?'

'No horse. And yes, all dead bad guys.'

'But I get the girl?'

'Uh-huh.'

'Lotsa dialogue an' stuff?'

'Not so much. You're the star.'

''Course I'm the star, ass-hole. Okay, I'll take it.'

The box went click. The dialling tone filled the room.

Both men sat back up from the desk. Menahem flashed a brief triumphant smirk at Larry. Then he glanced downwards at the steaming carpet littered with fragments of wet pottery and then looked back up and shouted across at the whole room,

'What is zis fuggin' shit? Can't do business in a shit-hole like zis. Less get to fuggin' vork, we got a fuggin' movie to make.'

He rose and walked straight out of the room, the delegation following.

I looked at George. He didn't look back. We listened to footsteps rapidly receding. In the silent aftermath I returned to the staff kitchen and found a bucket and dustpan and brush under the sink. The office was empty when I got back. I cleaned up as best as I could and took the ruins away. I locked up the kitchen and walked back and glanced back into the office. Still no George. I walked out and shut the door, leaving the lights on. I felt dazed, uncertain, as if I had just walked out of a plane crash, the sole survivor. I decided to go and find some lunch somewhere close by.

My favourite Soho kosher salt beef bar was close by. It had been rather a dramatic morning, and I wanted to find a familiar spot and get my bearings. I chewed my salt beef on rye with extra mustard ruminatively. I wondered if I was still employed by the company at all, in any capacity. At the end of forty minutes or so I decided I'd better go back and see George. If I skulked back to Miss Kaitlin at the Moulin it would look as if I was trying to hide my tracks. And anyway I wasn't officially on duty. So I strolled back into the Soho cinema again.

At the door stood a grizzled doorman in a long grey double-breasted uniform coat and peaked cap. He looked at my suit and at me.

'Ah, Mr Scudamore, isn't it? Mornin'. Mr McCann was hoping you might drop in. You're to go straight along. Do you know where to go?'

I nodded. Was he grinning at my back I wondered, as I went down the stairs? George's door was ajar. I knocked and waited. There was rather a pause and then a welcoming grunt. I pushed the door open and stepped in. George was behind his desk, putting the phone down. He had half a chocolate biscuit in his other hand. He gave me a long look and said,

'Well, how do you think it went?' His mouth was at a slant.

With a sense of inviting the apocalypse I asked faintly, 'Do I have a job?'

'Oh, aye. Stuart's a fair mun. An' Mr Jones has just bin on, y'know. He wants a proper tour, end o' next week. Ye'll have to be a wee bit more careful w' the crocks in future. Mrs Robinson is fair put out. Some of her best china lost...'

He grinned a reminiscent grin. Like air filling a vacuum the relief flooded into me.

'Sorry, and thank you and well, thank goodness...' I ended feebly.

'Oh aye. Stuart says that this Mr Menahem is so full of the new film he'll be makin' that he's no time for anything else. I'd guess Stuart has had a fair wee laugh over it all, but he'll no be sharin' it w'me.' He shot me a straight look. 'Or ye.'

The following Monday I started at the Soho Cinema properly. It was a strange environment because the only old hands on deck were the two projectionists. Mike and Henry had specific technical skills which would be hard to duplicate quickly. Not to mention a good, unionised contract which would make them very expensive to make redundant. The other staff had all been brought in at short notice from other branches of the company. As a rule the chance to change working positions, into a hall of supposedly higher reputation, is not something that happens often for cinema staff. So we all had a paradoxical sense of being all pioneers and yet, at the same time, of all entering a tradition with which we were not familiar.

Mrs Robinson had a silver-grey perm and tended to beige lipstick. She stood very upright and walked with a mature slink like a grandmother cat. She was very pleased with the tidy sales kiosk on the mezzanine. The kiosk had been modelled on the old-fashioned concession stands inside the Shaftesbury Avenue theatres. These theatres stood neighbours all along the street from the Soho Cinema. Accordingly the kiosk's stock range was conspicuously narrow and high-priced and did not run to smelly popcorn and smellier hotdogs. I believe Mrs Robinson's rather dignified presence rather helped sales; certainly she regularly moved an impressive amount of boxed chocolates and over-priced mints out of there.

John, the tall, grey-haired doorman, was to become a real friend over the next few years. He was from the west coast of Ireland and had seven brothers. In his tea breaks, in the staffroom behind the kiosk, he practised scales upon his flute assiduously, taking the reed out of the mouthpiece, so that he produced only a thin asthmatic wheeze of sound. He was a fund of tales of the West End cinema world, as seen from the point of view of queue management, having worked in and around Leicester Square since he had come out of National Service in the mid-1950s.

In the paybox were Elsie and Margaret. They were identical twins and had never married. They seemed to me like a single person who had two bodies. They lived together and preferred to dress alike. I never knew them to disagree with one another in the smallest degree. They had matching voices and gestures, and the effect could be a little disconcerting. I often wondered if they weren't mildly telepathic. In fact I hatched a vague plot to test this idea that involved giving just one of them a piece of information whenever she was covering Mrs Robinson for her break at the kiosk on the floor below. I would then race immediately upstairs to quiz the other sister. But I never quite found the right moment or, perhaps happily, the nerve to act on this scheme.

The Soho cinema really was a bit of an anomaly. It had been designed for an earlier era when prestige premiere releases would routinely run on a single screen for two or three months and indeed for very much longer if the title were notably successful. But the era of this style of release was effectively over already. The rise in home video, the increase in terrestrial and cable television channels, and the decline in average age of the mass cinema audience all had the effect of shortening the release cycle for new feature films. The studios now needed a far faster return on the huge investment that a new feature film represented. By now the global nature of much of the advertising for a film was a further accelerant. As a way of amortising the vast cost of promotion (on top of a film's production), the release and promotion pattern was becoming closely synchronised from release territory to release territory. This had always been implicitly so, but from the mid-1970s onwards the promotion of big releases was all explicitly planned, at an international level, almost like a series of overlapping military incursions.

In each national territory there would first be opinion-setting pieces planted in the big newspapers and glossy monthly magazines in the months before release. Then, in the two weeks prior to release, TV interviews on top chat shows and then, as the film opened, the stars would do a global tour over perhaps a three-week period, walking along a series of red carpets that stretched effectively from Hollywood Boulevard to Hong Kong's famed Canton Street. All of this effort was (and is) designed to provoke a climate of positive interest amongst as many different sections of the public as the marketing department can discern.

Perhaps the darkest urge behind all this frenzy of ever-increasing haste to the release pattern was the belief by the big studios in Hollywood and Bombay that they were losing a serious part of their income to video piracy. Films were being duplicated illegally, it was widely accepted, either in pirate labs or directly from the screen inside the cinemas, and then the resulting tapes were being sold to a thirsty and global public who were not, allegedly, deterred at all by the often considerable loss of picture and sound quality thus incurred. This audience often had less access to traditional cinemas anyway but, being exposed to the same global advertising, urgently desired the same paradoxical thrill of a brand-new film that would be at once as familiar as it was exotic. All over the world there is a common desire to visit, time and again, the bright and shiny world of cinema where the expensive foreign cars and the hair of expensive foreign women are equally lustrous. But who wants to wait for the same new film to roll its stately and legal way, in due turn, into one's tatty provincial cinema?

While I was at the Soho, that glorious auditorium had not yet been cut up into three smaller sets of halls to show a current trio of specialist titles. But not long afterwards it would be. Before then Cannon-Classic tried hard to fill the five hundred or so seats of the newly acquired Soho Cinema with either acquired new titles of sufficient grandiosity or to produce their own. Thus we had programmes that oscillated from *The Ballad of Narayama* to *Lemon Popsicle*. The former is a stately and heartfelt drama set in ancient rural Japan in which an elderly widow prepares for her own death, the latter an Israeli refry of *American Graffiti* of almost septic tastelessness. The year before the former film had won the Palme d'Or from the Cannes film festival while the latter had outsold every other rival comedy in Tel Aviv. In London, sadly, both sold few tickets, but perhaps for different reasons.

My special job, over and above throwing trays of tea over visiting dignitaries, was to programme late-night shows. To this end I concocted little late-night mini-seasons, in single or double bills, of directors or stars: I dedicated programmes to all my then current favourites such as Robert Bresson, Bob Rafelson, Werner Herzog and David Lean as well as to Sean Connery, Dirk Bogarde and Jack Nicholson. As part of these programmes I would also write programme notes in the style of the NFT: three-to four-hundred-word essays on the director or star of the current theme. In the main, however, attendances for these late shows were lamentable. Since I had previously had a very steady success rate with late-night single- and double-bills at the Paris Pullman only a few years earlier, I was very disappointed now. Perhaps, by definition, a big West End hall has no local following. And late-night transport for anyone who did attend was always notoriously limited. I felt very like a man who takes over a new shop lease and then stands in a clean white shirt, full of hope, behind his shiny new counter waiting for trade. But none comes.

And the main shows fared no better. With as much fanfare as the company could afford, Cannon-Classic launched exclusive engagements of *Koyaanisqatsi* and *Lemon Popsicle V*. We opened *Cross Creek* and *Love Streams* on exclusive runs with directors in attendance on the opening night. None of them created a stir with the general public – though a few earned some respectful reviews. Overall it was discouraging and so we began to feel discouraged. My brisk and hopeful weekly meetings scheduled with Stuart Hall, to discuss the current state of the late-night series, and to develop ideas for future themes, began to be pushed back. Then they were cancelled and re-scheduled. Then they ceased entirely. Meanwhile George McCann remained as professional as ever, and always captained a tidy ship. We were trim and sea-worthy, but we had no cargo. And then the wind began to leave our sails entirely.

Soon the rumours began. We were to be bought by another cinema chain. We were to be re-purchased by the original owners who had found a new and wealthier backer. The company we worked for was going bust at all of its halls. We were to become a bingo palace. We were to become a car park. A restaurant, a hotel, a casino, a supermarket... The fragments of pseudo information circulating amongst us became more and more eccentric.

Early one morning, as I was placing the security locks for the fire exits on their appointed board in his office, George called out from his desk, 'Nick, will ye have a seat? And close the door, please.' Immediately my heart sank. What stupidity had I committed now? What sin of commission or omission? The potential list seemed very long to me.

'Ye'll be remembering Mr Lucas from the Chelsea branch? He was here last week?' I nodded. I remembered shaking his hand.

'Well, he'll be askin' Mr Brown for a new assistant very soon, and I think you'd be wise to go and have a chat with him. I can't tell you anything but I'll be moving from here myself very soon, I fear.'

'Are we closing down, then?'

'Ah – that's no' fer me t'say. But you'd be well advised to pay a visit to Mr Lucas, that much I can tell ye.'

'Don't worry, I'll ring him now and see him this week. If you're sure...?'

'That'd be wise, then.'

George looked at me regretfully for a moment. The pitch of his voice changed as he went on, 'And tell Mrs Robinson to come and see me about her stock count – we seem to have misplaced a lot of mint creams this month. That's nay like her, nay like her a'tall.'

It was a classic case of that optimistic old nostrum: as one door closes, another opens. Only a few days later I went down to the Cannon-Classic Chelsea. Oddly, this house was well-known to me – as a punter. It was only a few minutes from my former childhood home. At the bottom end of the Kings Road Chelsea, the cinema had been cut into four screens back in the 70s and still did a steady trade. Oscar-bearing titles would begin in the larger auditoriums, then cascade down into the smaller rooms as their attendances declined. Speciality (i.e. subtitled) titles that had been well reviewed would often have longish steady runs of several weeks or more. The Chelsea was understood by head office to be a 'West End house'. This meant that although the cinema was geographically a good forty minutes by bus from Leicester Square, it nevertheless screened first-run product and was held under the command of the premiere release bookers in Wardour Street. Accordingly, the Chelsea was intended to be perceived as a prestige venue both by the customers who put their money down at the box office and by the staff who, effectively, drew their wages from it.

The Chelsea stood on a street corner that was not far from the river and was exposed to draughts from the north and east. Since there were no doors across the foyer in those days, the entrance was often unwelcomingly cold. Not that I noticed how cold the foyer was that day: since this was to be a meeting that was not explicitly an interview for a job I was preoccupied with trying to guess whatever might follow. The cashier politely took my name and then used the house phone. An usherette led me upstairs and along several brown corridors to a door. She knocked and a voice called to come in. She glanced at me but stepped well back. I walked in feeling a little as though I was jumping off a diving board.

Peter Lucas was an experienced manager who, like George McCann, had worked his way up to very near the top of the house management side of the company. From the handshake greeting of the week before I remembered a well-set man in late middle years with wispy white hair and a ready grin. Today Peter Lucas was indeed tending to stoutness and wearing a welcoming grin. He stood up immediately and stuck out a friendly hand. A crisp dry tug.

'So Mr Scudamore – how do you do? Can I call you Nick?' I nodded. 'How are you getting on with George at the Soho then, Nick?'

'Oh, pretty well I think. He's a fine boss and has taught me a lot that I probably should have learned quite a while ago. It's a beautiful house and he runs it very effectively.' I was conscious of being on my best behaviour. 'He's always after the cleaners and makes sure the sales area is well presented. He's good on staff punctuality, too.'

'A good man, George. So you get on with him?'

'Yes. He's a good boss, as I said.'

Peter Lucas smiled again. Had I imagined a spasm of embarrassment across his face? Then he motioned to an empty desk chair.

'Let's have a cup of tea. Milk and sugar? Yes? Hum. I won't be a moment.'

He turned and walked through a flimsy interior door at the back of the office. From where I was sitting I could make out a small storage area beyond fitted out with a very small table and an electric kettle on top of it. Peter busied himself. I looked round the office. Cluttered but not messy. That seemed encouraging. There were large peg-boards filled with work charts along the main wall. Most looked to be current. There was a pair of filing cabinets behind the manager's chair with a set of neatly labelled black ring-binders in a row on top. The opposite wall had a row of narrow windows that opened onto the noisy street below. Although it was markedly cool for a summer day, all four panes were open at the top. Accordingly, the traffic noise was quite loud. There was also, I was sorry to see, a largish ashtray on Peter's desk. It was half full of cigarette butts. There were two desks in the room, set to face each other. It reminded me of the orientation of police detectives' desks in the cop stations that you visit in the movies.

Peter strolled back in with two steaming mugs in his right hand. In his left was an open packet of biscuits. He plopped all three on the desk. The delivery hadn't quite the genteel polish of the Soho Cinema's Mrs Robinson, but it was nonetheless very welcome. Peter looked at me directly as he raised his mug.

'So how's business over there?'

'Not great. We are always hopeful, but I think Mr McCann is beginning to wonder why the company took on the lease of the place. If we've not got the product to fill it, I mean.'

'Yes. You're in a tricky spot there. What are your plans?'

'Well, to be frank, I've heard absolutely nothing about what Wardour Street is thinking about the future of the place. It would be a real treasure if it could be made to work. But perhaps I should be asking around – what do you think?'

'So you'd be willing to leave if you were invited? Here, for instance?'

'Do you think that'd be a good idea? You must have spoken to George McCann or I don't think I'd be sitting here. Would I?'

Peter grinned. 'Fair enough. Here's the thing of it. I think my assistant Mr Patel may be leaving very soon. And we're a busy house. I want someone who can deal properly with the class of customers I get here. And keep the staff up to the mark. And not panic in a crisis. We get all sorts here. Up the road is a big set of council flats. Not a job amongst the lot of 'em, poor sods. And at the same time I get lord and lady muck arriving by chauffeur from Knightsbridge, expecting a private entrance and a red carpet from their car door to their seats. Not to mention all the embassy diplomats and their wives. You know?'

I did. In time I was to see many representatives of all these cadres of humankind at the Cannon-Classic Chelsea, as well as many others beside. But for now it was time to shake hands and say goodbye. I travelled back to the Soho full of thought. It had been very considerate of George to give me this hint. It was not in the normal pattern of the career movements of cinema managers to take assistant managers with them whenever they moved on from a hall. If the Soho Cinema did indeed close I was more than likely to be left simply to fend for myself. But perhaps business at the Soho would pick up. It was a beautiful hall, in the very heart of the West End, well-maintained, with a good team operating it. I walked into the foyer and John, in his official brown overcoat, gave me his smartest wave-cum-half a salute. A nod to Margaret in the paybox. Down the elegant stairs to George's office. And walked straight in on George and Stuart Hall, deep in confabulation over the desk. The buzz of their conversation stilled instantly. They both looked at me.

'Sorry,' I said. 'I did knock.'

They clearly hadn't heard. Stuart rose, a little stiffly. Had he been here some time, I wondered? He turned to George.

'I'd better get back to the office.' He glanced at me, the corners of his mouth down.

'You. You'd better give me a ring. Tomorrow. Eleven o'clock? Right?'

'Tomorrow. Certainly. Is there…'

'Never you mind, young sir. Never you mind. Just give me a ring.'

He strode past me, out of the room. I realised only then how very fond Stuart was of a dramatic entrance or a dramatic exit.

George gave me a diplomatic look.

'Well, it's happened. Barry Jones and the rest of them have decided to try to find a buyer for this place. They've finally admitted they don't want to continue bankrolling us, just in hope of better things to come. It seems our new owners are using all the company money to finance the films they are going to make – and then we'll have nowhere to show the wretched things…' He snorted softly. 'He'll be tellin' ye ye've a month's notice to work out, would be my guess. How'd it go with Peter at the Chelsea?'

'Oh, we've an understanding, I think. But this is so sudden,' I said, feeling a bit winded.

'Aye. An' no. I saw it coming. To be fair Stuart was just here tellin' me the same advice I gave you.'

George smiled softly at the irony of this. He went on,

'There may be a slot for me at Oxford Street in a few months or so. Mr Richard's wife is very poorly and he's thinking o' taking early retirement, depending.'

And so it came to pass. Within three weeks I was leaving the lovely Soho – where I had started with such high hopes barely more than a year earlier, hopes I had shared with George, as well as some in the company high command, perhaps.

The MGM Cinema, formerly the Cannon-Classic, King's Road, Chelsea, 1992

Situated on the corner of Old Church Street and the King's Road, this auditorium opened as the Palaseum in 1910 but became the King's Picture Playhouse the following year. In 1943 it was renamed the Ritz and six years later the Essoldo. It was a Curzon cinema in 1972 but a year later it had morphed into the King's Road Theatre, home of the stage version of the Rocky Horror Show. It was converted to a multiplex by Classic Cinemas in 1980, taken over by Cannon and then by MGM before its demolition in 2018. A new purpose-built cinema opened in 2021 as part of the Everyman chain.

Local Studies and Archives, Royal Borough of Kensington and Chelsea

The Cannon-Classic Cinema, Chelsea, Autumn 1984

It was properly autumn by the time I started at Chelsea. The days were bright and cold, the tall plane trees along the Kings Road were shedding their brown leaves; the Christmas decorations were already beginning to bud out inside the shop windows. Peter Lucas was very welcoming.

When I came in that first Monday to be given the tour and a set of official keys he pointed to the cleared and gleaming desk opposite his own.

'Had the cleaners give it a wipe-over. Nice to start fresh, isn't it? You can put your coat over here.'

Through the narrow doorway at the back of his office I saw there was indeed a proper bentwood coat stand. I walked through to use it. There was the small table I'd seen before, and the kettle, but no sink or water supply at all. Under the table was a tiny fridge. The back of the area was just storage, and there were steps leading up to an area above the office.

By now all the re-established Cannon-Classic cinemas had adopted a uniform livery of gold, cream, and brown. We had brown carpeting on the floor with a wavy gold pattern and brown emulsion on the walls. The uniforms for the staff were the same colour. The particular colour combination had possibly been intended to suggest warmth and classiness. In practice it served mainly to disguise the almost universal grubbiness at so many of the company's sites. Peter worked hard at keeping after his cleaners to maintain standards but even so, heavy use and little investment meant that the surfaces all showed permanent signs of wear and tear very soon. The sales area in every house sold the same mainstream brands of confectionary and cigarettes at high prices. And very smelly steamed hotdogs. These were so full of preservative they tasted of nothing at all save the reeking yellow-coloured mustard that they could be dressed with. On Saturday evenings the smell of these implausible delicacies fought with the odour of the heated popcorn to fill the vestibule with a perfume that, oddly, never seemed to hinder the sale of tickets to enthusiastic queues.

At the Chelsea I had to accept a new rule. The manager never works on a Sunday. Peter always worked the Saturday evening with me – which was usually the busiest five hours of the week – so that was always welcome. But every Sunday he wished to be at home with his wife. The whole working week was sliced up to accommodate this preference. I certainly didn't work any more hours than was normal, but the timetable was not flexible. But at least at the Chelsea there were no 4.00am finishes, and so that was a real relief. A licence for late shows had always been opposed by the local borough council and anyway Peter didn't want to work them, so he always resisted any such suggestions from head office.

Peter had developed one side of the trade at the Chelsea to a very high degree, however. He used hard ticketing for all evening performances and throughout the weekend. For a local cinema to sell printed and dated paper tickets for a specific timed screening – exactly like a traditional theatre ticket – was, to my knowledge, unknown outside of Leicester Square premiere engagements.

The books of tickets, all calendar dated, had to be ordered from a specialist printer well in advance and were a considerable non-standard expense for the house. The administration for these was much more complex – remember this was well before the internet had come along to administrate almost every aspect of our daily lives – with a dedicated cashier having to respond to a dedicated telephone line so as to take bookings in advance, then having to take credit card details by hand over the phone and, later, to have the paper tickets ready for collection alongside the credit card hand-slide machine, ready for a signature to validate each individual sale. It was far from unknown for us to have pre-sold four capacity houses on Friday and Saturday nights, yet there was still a lot of queuing and signing and crowd management on such occasions.

With hard ticketing in a capacity house it is vital that usherettes lead people to their seats and make sure they sit in exactly their correct places. It takes planning and practice if it is to happen fluently. This was Peter's forte. Every Monday he would devise a precise timetable for the upcoming week so as to stagger the running of the film programmes through the entire up–coming seven day cycle, such that the projectionists could get from box to box and the usherette teams could circulate from hall to hall as efficiently as was humanly possible to manage the flow of customers. It is a significant organisational challenge to first rapidly take the ticket money from close to a thousand people, then sell them some sticky goodies, and then get them up the stairs and happily seated, all before their film starts, all the while allowing for the unpredictable vagaries of human nature.

For example: in the dense herd of customers climbing the stairs towards the auditorium –

'Oh darling, do go back down and get me some cigarettes from the stand, would you?'

Or

He: 'Got to use the loo, love, can I have my ticket?'

She: 'Oh dear, I'm SURE they were in my handbag – did you pick them up from the girl, darling? Oh, this wretched bag, I can't see them anywhere… (to usherette) Oh, my husband's gone off to the loo, but you'll let him in, won't you dear? Well, I HAD some tickets, of course I did. My goodness what a lot of people, but you needn't worry. (Looks behind) I say! Don't push…'

Or 'Has anyone seen Granddad? – he's wandered off again. Mummy, we can't sit down without Granddad. But I don't LIKE these seats, are you sure she's putting us in the right ones? She's foreign. Well, I can see it's sold out, but I would never sit this close, can't we move back, please, Mummy, pleeze…'

And so on and so on, ad infinitum. And the staff would be required to go through all this for all the screenings in all the halls for every successful film. Oddly, we didn't always need four blockbusters to sell out on busy weekends. If a group of friends turned up for a specific title and there weren't four seats together, they were as likely as not to take a quartet of seats in front of whichever title remained rather than abandon their outing all together.

The other great issue was smoking. Nowadays, in the English-speaking parts of the world at least, it is almost a folk memory that at one time almost all people smoked almost all the time in all public spaces without restraint. In the eighties this was already beginning to change. Public spaces were often divided, as far as was practical, into smoking and non-smoking areas: trains, planes, restaurants, even pubs had areas where the eccentric non-smokers could choose to be. Similarly most cinema auditoriums were divided into two areas: smoking and non-smoking. Where there was an aisle between the areas there was at least an identifiable physical division. That division was harder to believe in whenever there was literally no dividing space between the two sections, merely a notional line on a box-office seating chart. At the Chelsea we invariably sold out the non-smoking areas first in every hall, and so Peter petitioned head office to be allowed to declare all four halls 'non-smoking' and thereby increase the speed of sell-outs and prevent the occasional complaint that arose from a non-smoker being seated next to a smoker, as could easily happen during a capacity screening. But head office saw only a potential loss of revenue from tickets, not to mention the sales of our over-priced cigarettes. For years at every quarterly meeting of the circuit's managers, indeed on any appropriate occasion, Peter Lucas urged the powers above to make this change at the Chelsea because he was confident that the local public wanted it. But to no avail. Then one day in the late eighties Barry Jones saw a spreadsheet projection that showed just how much the annual fire insurance premium over the whole chain would shrink if all the Cannon-Classic halls were to be declared 'non-smoking'. And that did it. Upon an immediate diktat from Head Office the entire chain went non-smoking virtually overnight. The Chelsea certainly never lost so much as a single ticket sale from the change.

Peter had become a non-smoker himself not long before I started working with him. Indeed, that first Monday – of the freshly cleaned desk – I had noticed that the large dirty ashtray was nowhere to be seen. It seemed that his outgoing assistant had been a steady smoker and that this had been a minor but significant incentive for Peter to press him to pursue his career elsewhere. A lucky stroke for me and my wheezing chest, most certainly.

There were a few legendary runs for some titles at the Chelsea. In the year before I joined Peter, he reported he had done months of heavy business with Richard Attenborough's *Gandhi*. This film had the unusual distinction of being so long that it was screened with an interval of fifteen minutes. This had quadrupled the profits from the Chelsea's small, licensed bar area as well as hugely increased the ordinary sales. The hard tickets had also proved invaluable in this instance, the forward demand for the film having been unusually strong.

We had spectacular flops too, of course. Dudley Moore allowed himself to appear as the lead elf in something called *Santa Claus: the Movie* that had been planned by a big Hollywood studio as a huge hit that would be expected to be an annual re-issue to future generations of delighted kiddies. It died at birth. Despite a huge national advertising campaign it played to echoingly empty houses everywhere for the whole of its opening weekend. Peter was especially exasperated because that same Friday we had also opened a small budget English independent title which had been popped into the tiny 65-seater hall in the Chelsea's basement. This was sold out from its first screening at 2.00pm on the Friday afternoon. Each of the following screenings for the rest of the weekend were also sold out hours early. Consequently, we had to turn away throngs of potential customers during all the business hours of that weekend. Meanwhile Dudley Moore was dying of loneliness up on our largest screen. On the Monday morning Peter got on the phone to the head office bookers and raged about the business we were literally sending away down the street to our competitors. To his vast relief the change of hall was agreed that very morning and we swopped the two prints over there and then.

The beneficiary of the swop was the British title *My Beautiful Laundrette*. This was to do quite phenomenal business and ran for twenty-two weeks at the Chelsea before the returns dropped to the point where Cannon-Classic felt that the title had finally exhausted its local interest and withdrew it. This film is unusual in that its gay love theme does not become explicitly apparent until nearly an hour into the story. As the end credits rolled the clientele would stumble out through the auditorium doors heading down the stairs towards the street, buttoning up their coats, saying things like 'Wonderful, and such fun. I did enjoy myself, didn't you? But I certainly didn't know it was going to be about THAT... did you?' This frank surprise was expressed by half the people who saw the film, for nigh on half a year, as they tramped away along the brown corridor past the manager's office and towards the stairs and the front exit. Was this a triumph of wilful ignorance or self-congratulation? I could never decide.

Other films attracted particular sub-sets of humankind. One of the more memorable clans manifested themselves when we showed another well-reviewed independent, an American one this time: *Desperately Seeking Susan*. This is a feminine comedy of role-switching between the leading ladies, starring Rosanna Arquette and Madonna who was then on the very cusp of emerging as a significant film star over and above her already established global musical career. In the movie Madonna's character still inhabited her off-screen punkette persona, a demeanour and a costume still viewed as mildly radical at the time of the film's European release. Accordingly the cinema was also attended by many punkettes of the various Chelsea sub-varieties. Some of them were accompanied by slightly strained parents who were toting their thirteen-year-old offspring wearing way too much eyeliner and shredded lingerie. The kids looked pretty odd too.

We did capacity business that whole week and even on the second weekend, sold out at all four screenings. Early on the Sunday afternoon I was supervising the unusual sell-out for even the 1.30pm screening, sending the final bedraggled punkette fairies up the stairs to their anticipated delights, when I caught sight of a further two little poppets – in the required full Madonna-drag – standing disconsolately together in the vestibule. Neither of the pair looked to me to be even eleven years of age, despite the spectacular war-paint and fripperies. But both really looked their parts, the cutest pair of mini-Madonnas you could wish for. I walked across to them and bent down to speak.

'I'm sorry, my dears,' I said, 'we're completely sold out. But you could book for the four o'clock show perhaps…?'

The two of them gazed up at me gravely, then turned to each other, dumbfounded. Then one turned and looked back up at me very earnestly through her panda kohl eyes. In a tone clearly obviating the need for any further discussion she piped severely,

'But we're with Al Pacino.'

At that moment a tiny, rumpled man came round the corner into view. He seemed harassed and was certainly unshaven and uncombed. He was wrapped in a very expensive and very creased full-length cream-coloured linen coat. He appeared to be hiding inside it. He stood behind the two little girls looking quite as bedraggled as they. They turned to him, waiting for him to conjure this mere mortal out of their way.

'I'm sorry,' I said again, still looking down, 'but I really am full. I'd very much like to oblige you all but I can't before four o'clock, I'm afraid.'

My brain seethed. Here was the man I knew as Michael Corleone standing before me in the very flesh, and I was unable to accede to his request. He merely nodded to me and then smiled wearily down at the children and said immediately, 'Sorry girls, it's gonna have to be jus' pizza after all' and led them away by their hands.

Part of me wanted to run after him shrieking, 'Mr Pacino, take me away from all this, I revere you, honourable men go with honourable men, it's not personal Sonny, it's strictly business…' etc, etc. But the gods were not to be kind that day to either Mr Pacino or me.

Autumn passed into winter, and winter into spring. Martha and Ray separated for a while, and I found the atmosphere in her snug little flat becoming steadily less cheery. Nevertheless at the Chelsea I felt myself to be in a comfortable niche. Here there was a tolerant and professional boss, very steady business and a generally well-trained staff. All I had to do was to endeavour not to have too retrograde an effect on the whole operation.

There were convulsive disturbances in the rest of my life, however. One of my grandmothers decided to grant all her children and grandchildren a significant and equal capital sum as part of a general disbursement throughout her family. For me this windfall meant that, if I chose very wisely, I could arrange a mortgage on somewhere of my very own. A very small somewhere indeed, if that place was to be in central London. The flat I did eventually find was close by the British Museum. It was in a block that consisted of nearly three hundred and fifty tiny one-room units. Each flat was identical: a vestibule about four foot square, a tiny windowless bathroom with a sink, a tub, and a loo, and a main room only very slightly larger. Think of an old-style six-seat railway compartment and you have an idea of the scale. The kitchen was two shelves, a sink and a two-ring electric cooker installed inside a fitted cupboard. The two windows, facing north, were small, metal-framed and rectangular. From my fourth floor eerie I could see a small slice of sky above and a small slice of Russell Square below. The apartments were tiny but very well-built and warm.

I wondered if a 1930s builder or landlord had recognised the need in the area for rentable accommodation within the pockets of hotel chambermaids or railway workers or restaurant staff that might perhaps be working at the big hotels and rail termini that stand hard by that corner of Bloomsbury. The rooms made me think of superior student accommodation in a hall of residence. Once a floor to ceiling set of shelves had been built along my main wall and a sofa-bed installed opposite my tiny TV, I could think of nothing more that could ever be needed to perfect this snug little corner of paradise. I calculated that by restraining my intemperate taste for books and blank VHS tapes, I might be able to afford to pay my mortgage out of my £85.50 a week take home pay and pretend to be a grown-up at long last. This very first home of my own was an anticipated change of great excitement.

The death of my brother was not. He was an actor. Handsome, droll, a natural mimic, he moved with a lithe grace I always have lacked. His lop-sided smile could light a room. No matter how rumpled and unwashed he was, he always appeared trim and Byronically raffish. Slim-ankled women, their long hair smelling of patchouli oil, always swam devotedly in his wake. He was just beginning to have success, to collect reviews, to make well-received annual trips to the Edinburgh Fringe theatre season. Suddenly he was dead by his own hand. And none of us had had any intimation of this. In the following fortnight it fell to me to deal with the coroner's court, to make all the funeral arrangements, to guide my baffled parents and youngest brother through the quagmire of regulation and wider familial questioning. For five years my mother now would become effectively estranged from everyone and everything and even when she recovered enough to go on with her life the space that was her grief was never to be filled.

Exactly one week after the drear horror of Simon's funeral I moved into my shining new little home. My glee and my anticipation were sorely tempered by an acute sense of wrenching myself away from my parents at this sad hour. But I yearned to move on. These new streets around my new home were at once painfully familiar and enticingly new. Work was now a comfort, a soothingly routine constant. Yet every book or lampshade I had brought as a fond treasure from home was now tinged with nostalgic sadness. And every fresh scatter cushion or second-hand saucer that I brought into the new place seemed to glow as an emblem of the new. My breakfast sausage was cooked in a remembered pan, yet I tasted the mouthful from a brand-new fork. It was a very paradoxical time.

In the glum weeks after the funeral Peter was kind, and the staff at the cinema were very considerate. Many of the young men on the Chelsea's staff were Tamil. They would smile broadly at me each day, in a way they hadn't before. Their demeanour was as civil as it had ever been, but now, rather than the embarrassed half-smile which we English naturally wear for those bereaved, there were these wide smiles. I don't think these really registered with me as any odder than any of the other peculiarities of impression during that sad time. But a year or so later I was watching a documentary – on the war in Sri Lanka I think – and a BBC journalist was being led about the site of a wrecked village by the local headman. All about was utter devastation: ruined paddy fields, flattened trees, destroyed houses, litter, corpses. Yet the headman was smiling as he gestured. As the camera travelled across the faces of the villagers where this universal calamity had occurred, the women drew their head-cloths over their faces and turned away to face the rubble behind them. But the men, brown, thin-legged, exhausted, each straightened themselves upright and smiled broadly into the camera. My memory flashed immediately to those beaming faces I had met a year earlier, every day at work in the weeks after the funeral. Is it possible that the rictus of a half-embarrassed smiling frown that we here all so readily wear when faced with devastating sadness, especially on behalf of others, is but a learned cultural trope? That the expression we adopt at so quotidian an inevitability as death is not axiomatic but rather a habit acquired from watching our neighbours? Who knows?

Peter Lucas was as kind as ever. He had to allow me a few Sundays off now, but he did so with good grace. Eventually, however, life returned to close to normality. The cinema ran steadily on, we sold tickets to all sorts: Bob Geldof, Julie Christie, David Putnam, Tim Henman, Carol Thatcher and even a few un-illustrious others. Early one Sunday evening I was standing in the foyer in my regulation black bow-tie and dinner jacket costume, as company rules specified back then for all evening performances in 'West End category' houses. Business was very steady. We had sold out three of the halls already and the queues were still filing in. I was checking the crowds when I saw a stunning beauty standing just barely within the vestibule, well to the side, eyes downcast. Outrageously pretty women were not rare at the Chelsea, indeed the whole neighbourhood has long been famed for the models and actresses and wealthy county gals who have decorated the locale at least since Nell Gwynn so moved King Charles when she sold him an orange that he had a road made to ride to her. Poor thing, I thought, observing the blonde in the corner, she looks just like Princess Diana. She must have to endure quite a lot of bother from stupid strangers. Then I noticed the jug-eared fellow with a crew-cut and a big chest standing immediately behind her, exactly like a policeman in a suit. His eyes were traversing the mob ceaselessly, like a pair of range-finders. Like a slap I understood. This must indeed be Princess Diana gazing down at our grubby carpet while the mob swirled and her policeman stood guard. My heart hammered. There was a well-established protocol within the company for royal visits with the manager being warned well in advance and security and crowd control being closely supervised. Yet I was certain there had been no such advice from head office or anywhere else. That we were nearly sold out was also certain.

I divined that this must be an incognito visit and that if I approached her in my official uniform a fuss might arise. How to proceed? I held back and just watched the movement of the collecting line for reserved tickets. In a few moments an expensively dressed couple stepped away from the collecting queue, the man fanning a fistful of tickets. The smart pair now wove their way back across the foyer through the throng towards the blonde and her tame policeman. I tried not to make it obvious that I had observed the quartet as I watched for any recognition in the crowd. I badly wanted to get up to the office and phone Peter, but I felt it was more politic to stay in view and just watch that everything was running smoothly. The group of four began to make their way to screen number 1: *Crocodile Dundee*. Very popular choice, wise of someone to book ahead, I thought. I knew we had sold out for this title three hours previously. I followed along, going up several steps behind the four. Checking the hall as it filled would not be unusual for the duty manager. Indeed it is always wise for a manager to look in briefly, as a capacity house fills, if he can spare that crucial moment. This can often allay any confusions or small anxieties for either staff or customers as they arise.

Diana, her bodyguard, and her two companions were in the back row, the policeman on the very end seat, nearest the auditorium door. These were far from the best seats for viewing the screen but the group may well have had other priorities. Seeing that they were seated securely enough and that the usherettes were happily tucking in the last stragglers, I caught the nearest young miss and whispered, 'Katya, listen to me. Change of plan: stay here on the little seat inside the door. Don't move across to number 2 when this show starts. The house is completely full. Call me if there is any disturbance, any at all. Understand?' She gazed at me, not perturbed. Her job was now suddenly easier in a sense – she did not have to make the expected gallop to Screen 2 along with the rest of her team. The other three usherettes nodded as they passed us both by and exited to their next positions. All calm, it would seem. None had noticed. I was in a raging lather of anxiety, however. I shivered with the fear that something might, in some calamitous way, go wrong. The doors to the auditorium closed. The lights went down, the adverts and trailers started. I stepped out.

The projectionist – oh sweet Jesus – the projectionist! Was he cued up, was the aspect plate correct, the projector lens properly focussed, the sound level adjusted for a full hall? I nipped smartly up the stairs to the box for Screen 1. Young Ronnie was sitting on his stool by the peephole, with a comic open on his knee.

'Oh, hullo, Mr Scudamore,' he said sounding mildly surprised. 'Problem?'

'Not yet,' I hissed dramatically, 'but if you ever take your eyes away from the screen and have a mistake with this run I'll have you transferred to the night shift at the Leicester Square all-nighters for the next six months. Don't miss a single beat on this showing. Understand?' I glared at him. He stood up, the comic book falling to the floor.

'S'orl right, Mr Scudamore. Don't get in a panic. I'll watch. VIP, is it?' I rushed away pretending not to hear him mutter aloud to himself, 'Silly sod...'

Back in the corridor all sounded routine. The crowds were filing steadily into the other halls. I began to feel a little calmer. All was running as it should. I'd wait ten more minutes, until the last main feature had started, then go back to the office and phone Peter at home. I strolled along to Screen 2, taking deep breaths as I went. The hall was nearly full and the lights already down for the start of the main part of the programme, but there didn't seem to be any usherettes in here. There should have been four present – or at least three, given that I had glued one to her seat in Screen 1. Odd. But all seemed calm. Where had all those naughty ladies got to? At least no one had noticed our very grand customer and she had preserved her incognito, so all was well. I walked back along the corridor and round to the double doors in front of Screen 1.

The doors were wide open and all nine of the usherettes were jammed into the door frame, a tangled cluster of legs and backsides all protruding into the corridor. Their voices hissed like steam engines:

'Cor, are you sure?'

'Can't be her, can it?'

''Tis, I tell yer, look at 'er 'air... S'gotta be, innit?'

'Nah – we'd a bin told. Can't be. Yer daft, you are. She'd 'ave bodyguards, wiv radios, like. An' where's Charles, anyway, I'd likes to know...?'

'On a Sunday, too...'

The debate was becoming louder by the moment.

'Ladies!' I hissed behind them as loudly as I dared. As one the roiling phalanx of uniformed posteriors before me stilled. 'Oh heck, 's Mr Scu'more, innit...'

'Shush you lot. SHUSH, awl right...?'

They all turned towards me, flushed and rumpled, eyes glittering. Katya beamed at me.

'Oh, Mr Scu'more – there's Lady Diana in there. In number 1. Watching *Crocodile Dundee* – wiv some friends. Can we watch?'

They were all excited and perhaps a little abashed at their own enthusiasm.

It was a moment for me to try to sound managerial:

'No, ladies. She's just a customer on a private visit. Just like anyone else. She doesn't want to be stared at by the whole pack of you. Get back to positions or there'll be no early finishes for any of you this week at all. Please, ladies? Thank you all so very much.'

They went away, giggling quietly. Katya beamed at me as though I'd given her three birthday presents all at once. She slipped back into the hall and closed the doors behind her.

Nearly two hours later, just before the end of the screening in number 1, I too slipped into the hall, bringing two of the usherettes with me. They crept quietly down the sides of the auditorium to near the front of the hall, one on either side of the screen. As the screen finally faded to black and the very first frames of the end credits rolled upwards the crew-cut man leapt from his seat and stood in the aisle. Ushering his charge before him he led her immediately up towards the rear doors. In the dusk of the auditorium I caught a flash of her milk-white complexion and downcast blue eyes and she was past me and away. In another moment her two companions followed, encumbered with coats, out into the corridor beyond. I stood with my back to the closed door and, as the house lights came up, shouted to the audience to please leave by the fire exit down at the front. The usherettes pointed and repeated my command as they held open the fire doors. In five minutes the hall was quite empty. Someone had abandoned a rumpled copy of one of the previous weekend's Sunday broadsheets on a seat. I cleared the newspaper away. It was definitely time for a cuppa.

Back in the office I made the tea carefully, allowing it to steep properly, then carried the cup back to my desk. I picked up the slightly rumpled paper I had purloined, spread it out on the top of my desk and sat down with a small sigh of relief. Almost the whole front of the Sunday newspaper was given over to a carefully framed picture of Charles and Diana at some grand diplomatic dinner, seated stiffly side by side, resolutely looking away from each other.

The months wore on. I was familiar with all my routine tasks and performed them proficiently, if unremarkably. It has to be said that I was feeling underused, these days. The Chelsea was a well-run cinema with a good regular trade, and I had worked happily with Peter now for just over three years. A sense of routine can be comforting in that it can't co-exist in a world of stress. I wasn't discontented, but I didn't have a very clear idea of what I would like the next five or ten years to bring. I had the joy of a home of my own but I was definitely lacking something…

Earlier that year there had been another quite unexpected development, too. That spring I had fallen in love. I had met a slim green-eyed beauty who brooked no challenge. Within a few months we were both living together happily in my snug little cupboard of a flat. My parents were as delighted as I was amazed that such a thing could ever happen to me. Engagement followed. In the following spring of 1987 we were married, with much joyous to-do. Perhaps it was then, in the months that followed, that a sense of life's possibilities widening led me to feel rather more cramped at the cinema than I ever had formerly. Certainly there was also earnest and sincere encouragement from those green eyes. She believed I could teach. I was uncertain but pondering.

During all this I had to keep on working, however. Despite the promises of the poets you cannot live entirely on happiness.

Peter continually guided me towards honing my managerial skills. There was even a sounding-out as to whether I might like to take a junior post in the film-booking department at head office. But I demurred. I'd never quite liked the atmosphere in Wardour Street and felt uncertain about my chances of survival in any future round of administrative purges.

Friends elsewhere in my life had entered the world of teaching of TEFL – that is Teaching English as a Foreign Language – and described the profession as a steady employer. University friends reported having taken a four-week course in simple pedagogic theory and classroom method as well as in grammatical analysis of English. Then, duly certificated, they hoped to travel to some interesting part of the world where, with a little good luck, they could expect to earn just enough to keep them from starvation while they learned a little about another culture from the inside. I had no ambitions to travel, but there is always demand for English classes in London from a wide variety of international visitors, and work that put my education and my intellectual curiosity to some moderate use was certainly worth considering. I applied for a training course, took an admission test, passed and so was admitted to a training programme.

Now I had to go to Peter and tell him that I would be leaving in a month to begin a whole new chapter in my life. To me he expressed only a very little surprise. I knew full well that even the rumour of a slot possibly opening up as assistant manager at the Cannon-Classic Chelsea would mean that Peter would have plenty of candidates to select from. Almost all of them were quite likely to be rather better in the post than I had ever been. With excitement and trepidation I worked out my month. The staff were surprisingly fulsome in their several valedictions. In the final week I cleared my desk steadily, accepted many 'good luck' cards and felt increasingly distracted. Thursday was my final full day at the cinema, I walked up the road to the bus stop. My head was so full of thoughts about the new school on Monday – for I was to begin my TEFL training immediately – that I hardly noticed that along the King's Road the wind was stirring the tops of the plane trees in wide uneasy circles.

That night, for the first time in living memory, south-east England was struck by hurricane force winds and huge damage was done: cars were blown off bridges, sea-coast defences were overwhelmed, basement flats along some reaches of the Thames were flooded, old trees in all the royal parks and public gardens were blown down; even in central London the electrical power went down for several hours. That Thursday night we all slept little. On the Friday morning we emerged into a world of collective and civic bewilderment and, in many cases, tales of unexpected dangers that might have easily proved fatal. As I walked up the Kings Road that final Friday morning, I was awed by the sight of broken glass all over the pavement, by mature trees thrown down across the pavements, by parked cars bowled through shop windows. Everywhere little groups of strangers stood in shivering clusters sharing tales of the night and reassuring one another. The accumulative effect was sobering indeed.

At the cinema Peter and I made a full tour of the building and then even poked a ladder out of the projection box skylight and climbed out onto the roof to check for damage. There didn't seem to be any of consequence that we could see. Back in the office I shared a mug of tea and a biscuit with Peter, turned over my keys, and shook his hand for the last time. I would miss his smile, I knew.

Outside it was only midday but already the sky had cleared, and the warm air made the future feel inviting.